FAMOUS INDIANS
OF THE
20th CENTURY

Vishwamitra Sharma

V&S PUBLISHERS

Published by:

V&S PUBLISHERS

F-2/16, Ansari Road, Daryaganj, New Delhi-110002
 011-23240026, 011-23240027 • *Fax:* 011-23240028
Email: info@vspublishers.com • *Website:* www.vspublishers.com

Branch: Hyderabad
5-1-707/1, Brij Bhawan (Beside Central Bank of India Lane)
Bank Street, Koti Hyderabad - 500 095
 040-24737290
E-mail: vspublishershyd@gmail.com

Distributors:

Pustak Mahal®
J-3/16, Daryaganj, New Delhi-110002
 011-23276539, 011-23272783, 011-23272784 • *Fax:* 011-23260518
E-mail: sales@pustakmahal.com • *Website:* www.pustakmahal.com
Bengaluru: 080-22234025 • *Telefax:* 22240209
Patna: 0612-3294193 • *Telefax:* 0612-2302719

PM Publications
• 10-B, Netaji Subhash Marg, Daryaganj, New Delhi-110002
   011-23268292, 011-23268293, 011-23279900 • *Fax:* 011-23280567
• 6686, Khari Baoli, Delhi-110006
   011-23944314, 011-23911979

Unicorn Books
23-25, Zaoba Wadi (Opp. VIP Showroom), Thakurdwar, Mumbai-400002
 022-22010941 • *Telefax:* 022-22053387

© **Copyright: V&S Publishers**
ISBN 978-81-920796-8-4
Edition 2012

Printed at : Param Offsetters, Okhla, New Delhi-110020

Contents

POETS & WRITERS

ARTISTS

PHILOSOPHERS & THINKERS

FILM PERSONALITIES

SPORTING LEGENDS

MISCELLANEOUS

Preface

Undoubtedly the cradle of the first major civilisation, five millennia ago India was a fabled land where milk and honey flowed freely. Through the next few millennia, the land produced many noble souls who kept the country's rich spiritual and cultural heritage throbbing. From astronomy, mathematics and medicine to spiritual mastery and renowned universities, the land produced the best in all spheres.

Somewhere down the line, we lost our way, with complacency and inertia taking over, even as the world forged ahead and we were enslaved by different foreign invaders, including the British.

Centuries of serfdom, strife and struggle followed, as we sought to assert our identity and preserve the nation's rich cultural heritage. It was during this period of enslavement that countless inspiring personalities came to the helm, exhorting countrymen to awake from their slumber, throw off the foreign yoke and reclaim India's rightful place among the comity of nations. One man who inspired Indians and foreigners through his oratory was 19th Century legend, Swami Vivekananda, who once said: "First reform yourself before you reform the world." And a writer like Premchand used the written word as a source of inspiration.

Some of the most inspiring personalities lived during the 20th Century, a crucial period in the country's march towards independence. In this reawakening, individuals from every sphere contributed their mite: freedom fighters, politicians, social reformers, writers, artists and philosophers – even film and sports personalities. For instance, hockey wizard Dhyan Chand helped India whitewash all the white, supposedly superior nations during the Amsterdam (1928), Los Angeles (1932) and Berlin (1936) Olympics. India's stupendous gold run during this period dazzled onlookers, stunned opponents and silenced critics. It was moments such as these that had the nation glowing with pride, underscoring the fact that true genius couldn't be repressed despite centuries of cultural and imperialist hegemony.

Added to these were the inspiring examples of Gandhi, Tilak, Vinoba Bhave, Sri Aurobindo, Rabindranath Tagore and countless others who led from the front during the freedom struggle. Most Indian leaders eschewed violence, focusing on our ancient tradition of non-violent protest.

Once freedom was won, the war was still not over. Centuries of foreign domination had bankrupted the nation and its treasury and the 'Made in India' tag carried negative connotations. A new crop of individuals then came to the fore, ensuring the country did not lag behind in innovation and entrepreneurial spirit. JRD Tata, MS Oberoi, GD Birla, AB Godrej, Jamnalal Bajaj, Jagadish Chandra Bose, CV Raman, Homi Bhabha, Dhirubhai Ambani and others ensured that India's ancient spirit of enterprise was re-ignited. And a guru like Osho Rajneesh showed the path of spiritual freedom not just to Indians but also to foreigners.

Where once we did not manufacture even a safety pin, India is today the cynosure of all eyes with the world's largest pool of trained manpower. In many spheres, the 'Made in India' tag is now flaunted, not hidden – particularly in Information Technology. Where once Indian students aspired to study at Oxford, Cambridge, Stanford and other foreign universities, today the best foreign companies come to India every year for bodyshopping at the IIT campuses, vying for our best brains through stupendous packages!

In this amazing turnaround, hundreds and thousands of Indians have played a key role. Selecting only hundred-odd names has been an arduous task, with other equally deserving ones having been left out due to space constraints. This is not just a collection of achievements and milestones by select individuals – it is the story of an entire era.

I am grateful to M/s V&S Publishers for accepting this book for publication. Thanks also to Ms A Sunita Purushottaman for helping me in this endeavour. And grateful thanks to the editorial staff without whose untiring efforts this book would not have seen the light of day.

–**Vishwamitra Sharma**
C-3/58, Lawrence Road
Delhi – 110 035
Tel: 27194317

Freedom Fighters
& Statesmen

Mahatma Gandhi

Personality of the Millennium

(1869–1948)

Mahatma Gandhi shared the same disposition as Lord Rama, Lord Krishna, Jesus and Ashoka. In the entire 20th Century, there was none who could belittle Mahatma Gandhi's towering personality. But just as all luminaries come to earth with a purpose, Gandhiji came with the purpose of securing independence for India. It's a pity that though he delivered us from the bonds of servitude, he did not have the opportunity to enjoy the moments of glory. His dream of a united and strong India could not be fulfilled. It's ironical that Gandhiji did not live long enough to see the country stride on the path to progress. The simple man that he was, his immense charisma drew not only the rich towards him, but even inspired the poor.

There is no denying the fact that Mahatma Gandhi is the *personality of the millennium.* Gandhiji was born on 2 October 1869 at Porbandar, Gujarat. His father, Karamchand Gandhi, was the *diwan* (chief minister) of Porbandar. He was not a highly qualified person, but was a good administrator and knew his job well. Gandhiji's mother, Putlibai, was a deeply religious lady and she influenced him a lot. It was her piety and truthfulness that made him forsake and oppose vice. He would readily accept it if he committed any wrong. Gandhiji was brought up on the religious tenets of *Vaishnavism* (worship of Lord Vishnu) and Jainism. Both the faiths advocated the principles of *ahimsa* or non-injury to all living beings. So he was brought up on the principles of non-violence, vegetarianism and tolerance.

Gandhiji was an average student at school. Like every normal child, he had his share of childhood and adolescent escapades. But he resolved never to commit such transgressions and tried to improve himself. At the age of 13, he was married to Kasturba.

In 1887, he was just able to clear his matriculation from the University of Bombay. Then he joined Samaldas College in Bhaunagar (now Bhavnagar). He was not happy in college because he had to take up English instead of Gujarati. So when his family gave him the proposal of going to England to study law, he jumped at it. Thereafter, he sailed to "a land of philosophers and poets, the very centre of civilisation" in September 1888 and joined the Inner Temple, one of the four London law colleges. He took up English and Latin earnestly but it was difficult for him to adjust to Western society, especially because of his vegetarianism. But he met people like Edward Carpenter, GB Shaw and Annie Besant, idealists who were instrumental in shaping his personality and inspiring him to take up the role of leading the freedom struggle in India.

His mother died while he was in England. When he returned to India in July 1891, he tried to start his practice in Bombay, but failed to make a mark. So he moved to Rajkot and took up the job of drafting petitions for litigants. It was during this time that he had the opportunity of going to South Africa on a year's contract from an Indian company which was based in Natal, South Africa. It was there that he first saw how the coloured people were subjected to inhuman treatment by the white government. In one instance, when he was travelling to Pretoria, he was thrown out of a first-class railway compartment along with his baggage because he dared to occupy a compartment reserved for whites only. This incident led him to revolt against such inhuman practices and made him determined not to accept injustice and indignity.

Gandhiji tried to educate the people about their rights and duties. However, he had to sail back to India after the lapse of the contract in June 1894. He asked the people to protest against a bill that was to be introduced in the Natal Legislative Assembly to deny Indians the right to vote. The people saw a leader in Gandhiji, so they requested him to stay back. Gandhiji was never interested in politics and was afraid of public speaking. But the July of 1894 saw him metamorphose into an active political campaigner. He was just 25 then. Although he was not able to prevent the passage of the bill, he was able to organise a lot of support and got noticed by the press in Natal, India and England. The same year he founded the Natal Indian Congress to bring the Indian community under one banner. *The Times* of London and the *Statesman* and *Englishman* of Calcutta voiced grievances of the Natal Indians.

In 1896 he returned to India to take his wife and children to South Africa. On his return to Durban in January 1897, he was attacked by a white mob. When the question of punishing the guilty came up, Gandhiji refused to prosecute the wrong doers.

On the outbreak of the Boer War in South Africa in 1899, he raised a body of volunteers which included barristers, accountants, artisans and labourers. But his contribution was not recognised by the Europeans in South Africa. In 1906, the Transvaal Government introduced an ordinance that was particularly insulting to the Indian population. Gandhiji organised a mass rally in protest against the ordinance at Johannesburg in September 1906 and vowed to defy the ordinance and to accept any punishment. Thus was born *satyagraha* (appeal to truth). His struggle in South Africa lasted more than seven years. The Indian community too willingly supported Gandhiji and was not deterred from taking part in the struggle by the atrocities of the British. The end of the struggle came when the Governments of India and Britain intervened and the South African Government accepted a compromise.

Because of his activities in South Africa, not only was he a known figure in India but also familiar with the people in other British colonies. When he returned to India in 1915, he was acclaimed as an esteemed leader. The elite business class of India had formed an organisation called the Congress and they did not have any agenda except petitioning the British Government. Gandhiji's experiment with satyagraha in South Africa gave a new impetus to the freedom struggle in India. When he returned to India, not only leaders, even the Indian people welcomed him with open arms. The Indians found in Gandhiji a leader who acted as a buoy and harnessed the strength of the people for the independence struggle. But, his struggle for freedom in India was different from that in South Africa.

People of the whole country, irrespective of caste, creed and religion, became involved in Gandhiji's freedom struggle. With the Champaran, Rowlatt Act and the Khilafat Movements, he was able to involve the people from all over India and thus became the unrivalled leader of the Congress. His position in the Indian struggle was similar to the position occupied by Lord Krishna in the Mahabharata war. Even without wielding a weapon, the Lord steered the Pandavas to victory. Gandhiji was initially not a member of the Congress, but he became its lifeline.

After returning to India, Gandhiji met Indian leaders like Sir Pherozeshah Mehta, Lokmanya Tilak and Gokhale and toured the nation. His first satyagraha revolution was at Champaran in Bihar where the farmers were forced to cultivate indigo for the British. It was here that he met prominent leaders of Bihar like Rajendra Prasad and they also pledged their support to Gandhiji.

In August 1919, he stirred a nation-wide protest against the Rowlatt Act, which gave the British the authority to imprison without trial. Gandhiji launched a satyagraha and people all over the country participated in his struggle. In the spring of 1919 a gathering of around 4,000 people, who had collected for a meeting at Jallianwala Bagh in Amritsar, were fired upon by soldiers and several hundreds were killed. The whole nation was rocked by the incident and Gandhiji decided to call off the struggle.

By 1920, Gandhiji became a prominent national leader. He believed that it was because of our weakness that we were being ruled by the British. He launched the Non-cooperation Movement where he asked students to boycott government-aided schools and colleges and told people to leave government service. The response was overwhelming. In spite of large-scale arrests, the movement picked up. In February 1922, a violent mob set fire to a police station in Chauri Chaura killing 22 policemen. Gandhiji decided to call off the movement. He was arrested in March 1922 but was released in 1924 because of ill health.

Meanwhile, disunity between the Hindus and Muslims had crept in. Gandhiji tried to persuade the two communities to forsake their fanaticism. There was a serious communal outbreak.

Gandhiji then undertook a three-week fast in 1924 to arouse the people to follow the path of non-violence.

In 1927, the British Government appointed Sir John Simon to head a constitutional reform commission. The Congress and other parties boycotted the commission because it did not contain any Indian member. In 1928, Gandhiji demanded Dominion status for India at the Calcutta Congress meeting. In March 1930, he launched the Dandi March in protest against the imposition of tax on salt. Around 60,000 people were imprisoned in the nation-wide non-violent strike against the British.

In 1931, after talks with Lord Irwin, he called off the strike and agreed to go to England to attend the Round Table Conference. The conference was a great disappointment because it concentrated on the plight of the minority communities in India rather than the issue of transfer of power to the Indians.

Back in India, Lord Willingdon succeeded Lord Irwin. The new British viceroy tried to curb the growing influence of Gandhiji, who was imprisoned. In September 1932, he undertook a fast to protest against the attempt of the British to segregate the "untouchables" by allotting them separate electorates in the new constitution. A mass campaign was launched to stop discrimination against the "untouchables". Gandhiji called them "Harijans" (the children of God).

In 1934, he resigned from the leadership and membership of the Congress. He felt that the members had adopted the policy of non-violence for political reasons. He went to Sevagram, a village in central India, and concentrated on the uplift of weaker sections of society.

In 1939, the Second World War broke out. It was a crucial phase in India's independence struggle. Gandhiji wanted the British to withdraw from India. Gandhiji launched a massive campaign called the 'Quit India' Movement. There were violent outbreaks and an attempt was made to curb the movement.

The war ended in 1945 and the elections that ensued in Britain were won by the Labour Party. They decided to grant independence to India but the Muslim League wanted a separate state for themselves. Tripartite negotiations were held for the next two years between the Congress Party, the Muslim League and the British Government. In mid-August, there came a breakthrough in the talks when it was decided to partition India to form the Muslim state of Pakistan. With Partition came the mass exodus and massacre of innocent people on both sides.

Even before the negotiations were on, there was large-scale communal violence. The incidents pained Gandhiji. He immersed himself in the task of healing the scars inflicted by communal conflicts. In Calcutta and Delhi he was able to bring about communal truce.

Gandhiji used to organise prayer sessions. On 30 January 1948, when Gandhiji was being led to the prayer hall at Birla House in Delhi, he was assassinated by a Hindu fanatic Nathuram Godse. With 'Hey Ram' on his lips, he breathed his last. The symbol of peace, truth and non-violence was gone forever. His memorial at Rajghat attracts people from around the world even today.

Sardar Vallabhbhai Patel

The Iron Man of India

(1875–1950)

Sardar Patel played a major role in the freedom struggle, but the work he carried out after India gained independence is more significant. The map of pre-independent India had two colours – yellow and pink. The pink colour represented those parts that were under British rule, while yellow depicted those 556 small princely states that were ruled by princes and kings. These states were given the choice by the British to join either the Indian Union or the newly formed state of Pakistan after partition. They also had the option of remaining independent states.

After independence in 1947, Sardar Patel was appointed the home minister and he took up the arduous task of bringing all these princely states under the Indian Union. He did so through talks, conciliation, appeasement, use of money and even force. Soon, all the princely states merged into the Indian Union. Only the Nizam of Hyderabad created a problem, but the use of police action made him comply with the wishes of Sardar Patel. This was how a strong India was formed. The work seemed impossible, but Sardar Patel displayed immense shrewdness and temperament and was successful in achieving his aim. It is because of this reason that he is called 'The Iron Man of India'.

Sardar Patel was born on 31 October 1875 at Nadiad in Gujarat, into a family of well-to-do landlords of the Leva Patidar caste. Being the fourth son of the family he always remained neglected, but he had strong will power. Sardar Patel married at the age of 16. He desired to go to England to study law, but his family was not able to bear the expenses. So after his matriculation at the age of 22, he cleared the district pleader's examination, which helped him practise law. In 1900 he established an independent office of district pleader in Godhra and later moved to Borsad in Kheda district of Gujarat. His wife died in 1908 and he remained a widower. They had a son and a daughter.

In 1910 he went to London to study at Middleton. After clearing the examinations with flying colours, he returned to India in February 1913. He started his practice at the Ahmedabad bar and soon became a renowned barrister in criminal law. He was also known for his mannerisms and western style of dressing, was good at bridge and a member of the fashionable Gujarat Club.

It was in 1917 that he was first drawn towards Indian politics. It was during this time that Gandhiji entered politics. Gandhiji was particular that educated people of each region should be a part of his movement. In Bihar, he took Dr Rajendra Prasad and other lawyers into his fold. In Uttar Pradesh, he was closely associated with the Nehru family. In Gujarat, Gandhiji came across Sardar Patel. After their association with Gandhiji, all the leaders gave up their flourishing practice and joined the freedom struggle. The Sardar was deeply influenced by Gandhiji and his satyagraha movement. Though he did not support Gandhiji's policies wholly, he resolved to support Gandhiji. He gave up western clothes and dressed in white kurta and dhoti, clothes of the Indian farmer. He also quit the Gujarat Club.

He became the first Indian municipal commissioner of Ahmedabad in 1917. He held the post till 1924 and then became its elected municipal president from 1924 to 1928. In 1918 he planned mass rallies by organising the peasants, farmers and landowners of Kaira district to protest against the decision of the Bombay Government to collect the full annual revenue taxes in spite of crop failures caused by heavy rains. In 1928, he led the landowners of Bardoli in their protest against increased taxes. This was a successful campaign and it earned him the title of *sardar* (leader).

Like all political leaders he too had an independent point of view. In the early years of the freedom struggle, he believed in acquiring Dominion status for India rather than complete independence. Unlike Pt Nehru, Sardar Patel believed that armed revolution should be avoided because it would entail severe repression. And unlike Gandhiji, he did not believe that Hindu-Muslim unity was a prerequisite for independence. Sardar Patel had imbibed traditional values from his family so he did not believe in adopting a socialist pattern for India.

In the Lahore session of 1929, Sardar Patel was the second candidate after Gandhiji for the post of the presidency. Gandhiji opted out of the candidature because he did want the session to adopt the resolution for independence. He also forced Sardar Patel to withdraw because the latter opposed Hindu-Muslim unity. So Pt Nehru was elected the president of the session. In 1930, during the salt satyagraha, he was imprisoned for three months. Sardar Patel presided over the Karachi session of the Congress in 1931. He was arrested the following year in January only to be released in July 1934. After his release he campaigned vehemently for the Congress during the 1937 elections and was the main contender for the presidency of the 1937-38 session of the Congress. Again because of the intervention of Gandhiji, Sardar Patel withdrew and Pt Nehru became the president. Sardar Patel always acted with prudence and tact and accepted Gandhiji's wishes with diplomacy and always remained steadfast behind Pt Nehru. In October 1940 he was imprisoned along with other Congress leaders and released in August 1941. He was again imprisoned between August 1942 and June 1945.

When the Japanese attacked India during World War II, he rejected Gandhiji's non-violence. He opined that partition was in the interests of the country. Again because of the intervention of Gandhiji, in spite of being the leading candidate, Sardar Patel was not able to become the president of the Congress. Pt Nehru became the president of the Congress and he was invited by the British viceroy to form the interim government.

In 1947 India became independent. But the country was partitioned to satisfy the ideals of Jinnah and the Muslim League. Apart from Hyderabad and Junagadh, a few other princely states had Muslim rulers. Thanks to the efforts of Sardar Patel, they agreed to join the Indian Union. But the situation in Kashmir was different. Firstly, Kashmir shared its boundaries with Pakistan. Secondly, the people of Kashmir Valley were mostly Muslims, but the ruler was a Hindu. The ancestors of Pt Nehru were Kashmiris, so he looked after the affairs of Kashmir. Seeing the sensitive situation in Kashmir, Pakistan attacked Kashmir. It was then that Maharaja Hari Singh decided to accede to India. When he signed the pact, the army was sent to Srinagar to rescue the state from Pakistani tribals who had infiltrated into Kashmir. Before the tribals and the Pakistani army were evicted from Kashmir, a ceasefire was declared. So almost one-third of Kashmir was usurped by Pakistan.

Even after 1947–48, Pakistan attacked India twice and has indulged in clandestine warfare ever since. It trains young boys to disrupt the stability and unity of the country. The Kargil war makes it evident that Pakistan is trying to acquire Kashmir by hook or by crook. The only excuse they have to do so is that the majority of Kashmiris are Muslims. Some politicians believe that if Sardar Patel had been handed over the matter of Kashmir, the situation would have been in our favour today. When it came to decision-making, unlike Pt Nehru, Sardar Patel displayed sheer grit and determination. His one ambition in life was to have a united India.

After Independence, he worked for the welfare of the country with great enthusiasm. But the assassination of Gandhiji was a big blow for him. He had an undying love for Gandhiji. He considered Gandhiji as his elder brother and guru.

Between 1947 and 1950 he was the deputy prime minister, minister of home affairs, minister of information and minister of states.

On his death on 15 December 1950, the whole nation was plunged into grief. What Sardar Patel did in the 20th Century to unite the whole of India is unparalleled. Had it not been for Sardar Patel, India would still have been in fragments.

Bhagat Singh

The Great Revolutionary

(1907–1931)

India's freedom struggle was based on two schools of thought: the policy of non-violence advocated by Gandhiji and the extremist way – the seeds of which were sowed in the First War of Independence of 1857. Around the time the Congress launched the freedom struggle, a new generation of revolutionaries arose and their representative was Bhagat Singh.

Many Indians drew inspiration from the revolutionaries and were enthused by the idea of participating in the freedom struggle. And Bhagat Singh was the prime inspiration behind this feeling. The entire family of Bhagat Singh was involved in the freedom struggle. His father Kishan Singh was imprisoned for nationalist activities when Bhagat Singh was born. His uncle Sardar Ajit Singh had already been exiled for anti-British activities.

Bhagat Singh was born in September 1907 in Banga village (now in Pakistan) of Lyallpur district. His father was released for a few days from prison to see his newborn son. Bhagat Singh's early education was imparted in the village. Then he was sent to Lahore. In 1921 when the Non-cooperation Movement began, he was admitted to the National College where Punjab Kesari Lala Lajpat Rai, Bhai Parmanand and other patriotic leaders taught. On the insistence of Gandhiji, many students left government colleges. One of Bhagat Singh's classmates was Sukhdev, who was later a co-accused in the Bombay incident and was hanged along with him.

When Bhagat Singh was studying in college, his parents decided to get him married. Bhagat Singh ran off to Delhi, leaving behind a note saying that he was going off because he did not want to marry, and that they should not worry.

Bhagat Singh worked as a correspondent at *Dainik Arjun* in Delhi. Later, he went to Kanpur and worked for *Pratap*, a daily published by Ganesh Vidyarthi. It was here that he was introduced to Batukeshwar Dutt. During those days the rivers Ganga and Yamuna had caused great havoc in Kanpur. So these young men joined hands to serve the victims of the flood. It was here that Bhagat Singh met Chandra Shekhar Azad. Bhagat Singh was convinced that the country could gain independence only through revolution. So he established the *Naujavan Bharat Sabha* in 1924. Bhagat Singh, Sukhdev and Bhagwaticharan signed the declaration with their blood. To test the will power of the young members, Bhagat Singh placed his hand above the flame of a candle for 20 minutes. The flesh of his palm burnt and his compatriots had to forcefully remove his hand from the flame.

The people of India opposed the Simon Commission, so when it arrived in India, it was received with black flags. A band of peaceful protestors, which held a demonstration in Lahore, was clubbed mercilessly. Lala Lajpat Rai was gravely injured in the lathi-charge. He remained critical for a few days and then succumbed to his injuries. Bhagat Singh, Sukhdev and Rajguru killed the English officer Saunders who had hurt Lalaji.

In 1930, Bhagat Singh and Batukeshwar Dutt threw bombs in the Delhi Assembly, when the Public Safety Bill was being introduced. The Bill proposed to end the rights of workers to strike. Bhagat Singh and Dutt shouted slogans *Inquilaab zindabad* ("long live the revolution") and courted arrest. They were charged with many offences. Bhagat Singh, Sukhdev and Rajguru were found guilty in the Lahore bomb incident, the killing of Saunders, and the Assembly bombing case and sentenced to death.

In jail, Bhagat Singh and many of his associates went on a hunger strike demanding better conditions in prison. Bhagat Singh fasted for 115 days but Yatindra Das passed away on the 63rd day of the hunger strike. The large-scale agitation finally forced the government to concede their demands. On 23 March 1931 Bhagat Singh was hanged along with Sukhdev and Rajguru. The three patriots embraced death gallantly with the National Song on their lips.

Pt Jawaharlal Nehru

The First Prime Minister of India

(1889–1964)

India's first Prime Minister Pt Jawaharlal Nehru is considered the chief architect of modern India. He was the prime minister for 17 years, apart from the years he devoted towards India's freedom struggle. Pt Nehru's most significant contribution was to provide stability to parliamentary democracy. It is because of his efforts that our law-making body and the Press are independent, the bureaucracy does not interfere in politics and the role of the army is restricted to protecting the nation. Compare our state of affairs with that of Pakistan, which has faced a number of military coups and, after more than 50 years of existence, is still ruled by the army.

Jawaharlal Nehru was the son of Pt Motilal Nehru, a prominent lawyer of Allahabad and a leader of the independence struggle. Young Jawahar was educated at home by English tutors till the age of 16. In 1905, he was sent to Harrow. After two years at Harrow, he joined Trinity College, Cambridge for an Honours degree in Natural Science. By the time he left Cambridge, he had also earned a degree in law.

In March 1916, Pt Nehru married Kamala Kaul. Their only child, Indira Priyadarshini, was born on 19 November 1917. After his return from England he pursued law. But he found himself out of place in the company of lawyers. Like his peers, he wanted to take part in the freedom struggle.

Pt Nehru met Gandhiji for the first time in 1916 at the annual meeting of the Indian National Congress in Lucknow. Pt Nehru joined the Congress in 1919 just after the First World War. In 1921 many prominent freedom fighters were imprisoned. Pt Nehru went to jail for the first time then. During the freedom struggle he served nine periods of detention, which amounted to more than nine years in prison, the longest being the last, an imprisonment of three years that ended in June 1945. In 1923 he became the general secretary of the Congress for two years and again in 1927 for another two years. It was during those times that he was actually able to gauge the level of poverty and degradation of agriculture in India. This was to help him during his prime ministerial days ahead. In 1926-27, he toured Europe and Russia. He was deeply influenced by socialism and Marxism. During his imprisonment he was able to study Marxism in depth.

The Congress demanded Dominion status for India. In 1929, Pt Nehru was elected as the president of the historic Lahore Session that demanded *Purna Swaraj* (complete independence). This saw the emergence of Pt Nehru as the leader of the country's intellectuals and the youth. After his father's death in 1931, Pt Nehru became closer to Gandhiji. The Indians began to view him as the political heir of Gandhiji though Gandhiji himself did not officially designate him so until 1942. In March 1931 after the Gandhi-Irwin pact was signed, it was believed that peace would prevail between the Indians and the British. These hopes died when Lord Willingdon took over as the new viceroy. Gandhiji was arrested in January 1932 just after he returned from the Second Round Table Conference in London. Pt Nehru was imprisoned for two years.

India was given the right of self-governance under the Government of India Act 1935, which was the direct result of the Round Table Conferences. In early 1936 Kamala Nehru was taken to Europe to cure her illness but she died later in a sanitarium in Switzerland. Europe was reeling under the Second World War. Pt Nehru insisted that India would support England and France only as a free country.

The Congress Party came to power in a majority of states in the 1937 elections after the introduction of provincial autonomy under the Act of 1935. The Muslim League fared badly and their plea for the formation of coalition governments was rejected. This created differences between the Congress and the Muslim League, which later led to the partition of the country.

In September 1939, India was committed to the Second World War. The autonomous provincial ministries were not consulted, so the Congress withdrew its ministries as a mark of protest. Opinions differed on the subject. Gandhiji believed that the British should be supported unconditionally and any protest should be of a non-violent nature. Pt Nehru believed that in the war against Nazism, India should support the British only as a free nation.

In 1940, Pt Nehru was arrested and sentenced to four years' imprisonment. In 1942, when Japanese forces under the command of Netaji Subhash Chandra Bose reached the borders of India through Burma (now Myanmar), the British felt threatened. Sir Stafford Cripps, a member of the War Cabinet, was sent to India to initiate talks and bring about a settlement of the constitutional problem. The mission failed because Gandhiji wanted nothing short of independence. The Congress passed the Quit India resolution in Bombay (now Mumbai) on 8 August 1942. Gandhiji, Pt Nehru and the entire working committee of the Congress were arrested. Pt Nehru was released from his ninth and last detention only on 15 June 1945.

The Second World War came to an end in 1945. The Labour Party assumed power in Britain and sent a Cabinet Mission to India. Lord Mountbatten replaced Lord Wavell as the viceroy. No amicable solution could be reached, so the partition became inevitable. Much against the wishes of Gandhiji the country was partitioned into two independent countries – India and Pakistan. Pt Nehru became the first Prime Minister of India.

Gandhiji chose Pt Nehru as the president of the Congress at the 1929 Lahore Session. The attitudes of the two leaders were contrasting. Gandhiji had a religious bent of mind and wanted Indians to feel proud of India's past glories. Pt Nehru had a modern approach and a dream – to make India a self-reliant modern country. He wanted ancient thoughts, beliefs and traditions to co-exist with modern ones. This was because he had studied the history of developed countries and their political progress from close quarters during his Harrow days. So he was aware of the progress of science, technology and the economy.

Pt Nehru played a significant role in chalking out the direction of Indian politics and the Constitution. He wanted India to be a secular country. In spite of being a country with many castes, creeds, religions and languages, the people of the country are woven into the national fabric like yarns of different colours. Pt Nehru adopted modern values and ways of thinking and adapted them to suit Indian conditions. He wanted to carry India forward into the modern age of scientific and technical development. Pt Nehru felt the necessity of social concern for the poor and the underprivileged. And towards this effort the ancient Hindu Civil Code was reformed. This enabled Hindu widows to enjoy equality with men regarding matters of inheritance and property.

Pt Nehru's modern outlook attracted the younger intelligensia. He built a number of industries and dams for the progress of the country. He called them 'pilgrimage centres'. Pt Nehru developed public sector units so that capitalists of the country did not have a hold on the financial markets.

Partition brought with it a number of problems. Kashmir became a perennial problem. In 1948, Pakistan made an unsuccessful attempt to annex Kashmir. Pt Nehru was able to rid the country of Portuguese occupation of Goa. Another one of them was the Chinese aggression of 1962. Tibet was between China and India and it was given the status of a 'buffer state' by the British. The coining of the slogan 'Hindi-Chini Bhai-Bhai' and good neighbourly relations with the Chinese did not deter them from attacking India and occupying some parts in the north. Pt Nehru had blind faith in the Chinese but they had other intentions.

Pt Nehru's health showed signs of deterioration soon after the Chinese aggression. He suffered a mild stroke in 1963. In January 1964 he suffered another stroke. He died on 27 May the same year following a third and fatal stroke.

Some people believe that if Pt Nehru had not been in politics, he would have made a good historian or writer. Apart from his Autobiography, *The Glimpses of World History*, and *Letters to My Daughter from Prison* are significant works. Pt Nehru loved children very much. They called him "Chacha Nehru". Every year Children's Day is celebrated on 14 November, his birth anniversary.

Netaji Subhash Chandra Bose

The Fiery Revolutionary

(1897–1945)

Subhash Chandra Bose was a national leader who was faithfully associated for many years with the Congress party that followed Gandhiji's path of non-violence, but when he saw the atrocities of the British Government and the plight of the people, he chose a path totally different from Gandhiji's school of thought. He believed in the saying, 'An eye for an eye' and 'a tooth for a tooth'. And to rid the country of the British, he formed the Indian National Army (INA) or the Azad Hind Fauj.

The INA was an excellent example of social equality. The army consisted of people from different religions. But the spirit that united them all was their desire to release India from the bonds of slavery. The British Government was propagating the 'Divide and Rule' policy at that time. But Subhash Chandra Bose's efforts in forming the INA was a blow to the British policy and a symbol of national pride. And he set this example at a very young age.

When Bose was studying in school, the prevalent thought was that British children were superior to their Indian counterparts. The making of a revolutionary was witnessed when he beat an English boy in school to protest against this discrimination. When he was just 15, he told his mother that India was God's favourite country. He kept this thought kindled in his heart till the end of his life and also urged his followers to keep their solemn faith in India. He was of the opinion that no country in the world had the power to keep India in fetters for long. He had faith that India would soon gain independence.

Bose was born into a wealthy family in Cuttack. After completing his studies in India, he went to England to appear for the Indian Civil Services Examination. He cleared the examination and returned to India. But because of his patriotism, he gave up the ICS and joined the struggle for freedom.

Netaji Subhash Chandra Bose occupies a unique position in the history of India's struggle for independence. Though a member of the Congress, Bose took a different path in his struggle for Indian independence. The whole nation was excited when it learnt that Bose had gathered a large force to challenge the British and declare war to win India's independence.

The incident happened in 1940. There was a memorial named Dalhousie Square in Calcutta. The British claimed that in the First War of Independence in 1857, the Indians had burnt the hall after stuffing it with English men, women and children. The story, however, did not hold any water. This was an attempt to malign the Indians. Subhash Chandra Bose started a campaign to put an end to this memorial. Bose and his associates were imprisoned. Seeing the wrath of the Indians, the memorial was removed, but Bose was not released from prison.

In protest against the atrocities of the British, he went on a hunger strike on 20 November 1940. The British Government panicked and he was released from prison. But he was placed under house arrest amidst tight security. From then onwards Netaji's struggle for India's independence became famous.

The Second World War was on. But nobody could read Netaji's mind. During the house arrest, he grew a beard. This helped him disguise himself as a Pathan and flee from the clutches of the British to Peshawar. In Germany, Hitler was on his victory trail. Bose believed that it was best to befriend the enemy of one's enemy. So he met Hitler and sought his help. But it was difficult to fight for the cause of India from Germany. So after some time, he reached Japan in a submarine. He believed that Gandhiji's policy of non-violence could not help India in achieving freedom. So he founded the Indian National Army. He received the co-operation of Indians settled in Burma, Singapore etc. He called on patriots and said, "Give me your blood and I'll give you freedom." In February 1944, he had his first success. He was able to instil a sense of pride and devotion for India so that people were ready to make sacrifices for their homeland.

But the INA was not successful in liberating India. One of the major reasons was that in the predominantly marshy and thickly forested region, the weather led to the spread of malaria among the soldiers. Japan had to surrender to America after the latter used atom bombs. In Europe, Germany was defeated by the Allied Forces. The INA was successful in reaching Imphal. But because of the fall of Hitler, whom he considered his ally, Bose's dream of liberating India could not be successful. It is believed that he later died in an aircrash in Taiwan in 1945.

Jayprakash Narayan

The Lok Nayak

(1902–1979)

Jayprakash Narayan's life was different from the lives and times of ordinary leaders. When Indira Gandhi declared national Emergency, he was taken aback. He remained in hiding and organised a mass movement called the JP movement, aiming at total revolution. JP played a very significant role in the Quit India Movement. He led the movement heroically and successfully in Bihar, as a result of which the government lost all control over administration.

Jayprakash Narayan is among the few leaders who have received the respect and love of the masses. All through his life, he shied away from seeking a position in the government although he came across ample opportunities. Pt Jawaharlal Nehru offered him a place in his Cabinet, but he politely declined. After Pt Nehru's death, his name was proposed for the vacant position. Even when an opportunity to become the President of India arose, he put forward the name of Dr Zakir Hussain. He held the belief that once he had made up his mind to stay away from power, there was nothing that would lure him towards it.

Among many of his significant works was the solution that he found to solve the problem of the dacoits of Chambal. They created havoc in Chambal and the adjoining areas and were a constant headache to the government. Jayprakash Narayan was able to persuade them into surrendering before the government.

Jayprakash Narayan was born in Sitab Diyara village, about 50 km from Patna, the capital of Bihar, on 11 October 1902. He was the fourth child of Arsu Dayal and Phoolrani. His early education was completed at the village school. His nationalist feelings were strong even when he was a teenager and he took to wearing khadi. He completed his intermediate from Bihar Vidyapeeth.

At this moment in life, he was not sure about his future plans when he was married to Prabhavati, the daughter of a prominent leader Brijkishore. He was then 18 years old and she was only 14. As she was very young, she was not sent to her husband's place, instead she was sent to Sabarmati Ashram to stay with Gandhiji and Kasturba Gandhi. Then he enrolled at California University in America. In the seven years that he spent abroad, he was deeply influenced by Marxist philosophy.

When he returned to India in 1929, he was faced with a strange dilemma. He met his wife at Gandhiji's ashram. She was influenced deeply by the thought of celibacy during her stay at the ashram. Jayprakash respected her sentiments, and in spite of being husband and wife, both practised celibacy.

On the political front, he joined the Congress in 1929. When he came over to Allahabad from Bihar, he came in contact with Pt Nehru. In 1932, he was imprisoned in Nasik Jail for one year for his participation in the Civil Disobedience Movement. There he came in contact with Ram Manohar Lohia, Minoo Masani, Achyut Patwardhan, Ashok Mehta, Yusuf Meherali, Morarji Desai and other national leaders. When he was released, he formed the Congress Socialist Party, a left-wing group within the Congress.

In 1939, he was again imprisoned for protesting against Indian participation in the Second World War, but he escaped. He tried to rally the masses against British rule but along with his revolutionaries he was arrested in 1943. He wanted the Congress to adopt a militant policy against the British.

After India gained independence, JP formed the All India Congress Socialist Party along with Acharya Narendra Dev. In 1953, he helped in the merger of the Krishak Mazdoor Praja parties. In 1972, he came in contact with Vinoba Bhave and joined Vinoba's *Bhoodan* Movement. It was during this time that his wife died of cancer. Though it was a big loss for him, he continued to serve the people.

He shot into prominence in 1974, when he openly criticised the Congress Government for misrule and large-scale corruption. In 1975, when the Allahabad High Court convicted Indira Gandhi for resorting to corrupt electoral practices, JP called for her resignation. However, Indira Gandhi declared a national Emergency. JP and other prominent leaders were arrested. When he was released after five months, his movement against corruption, called the JP movement, gathered momentum. He was able to unite different political parties like the Jan Sangh, the Socialists, the Congress (O) and the Bharatiya Lok Dal under a new banner – the Janata Party. In the 1977 elections, the Janata Party was able to rout the Congress to form the first non-Congress government after Independence. Though his was the most important contribution, he stayed away from power and let Morarji Desai take over the reigns of the government.

Soon his health deteriorated and he had to be kept on dialysis. On 8 October 1979 he died. He was honoured with the Bharat Ratna posthumously in 1999.

Lokmanya Tilak

The Spirit of Swaraj

(1856–1920)

It is necessary to include Lokmanya Bal Gangadhar Tilak in the list of famous Indians of the 20th Century because it was largely due to his efforts that the feeling of pride and self-respect was aroused among Indians. He never believed in the policy of pleading for one's rights. He was the one who formed the extremist wing of the Congress because he believed in acquiring rights by force. And the thought had many takers. Among his supporters were Bipin Chandra Pal and Lala Lajpat Rai. And the triad – Lal, Bal, Pal – supported the extremist wing of the Congress. It was Tilak who coined the slogan "Swaraj is my birthright."

Bal Gangadhar Tilak was born on 23 July 1856 in Ratnagiri district of Maharashtra. His father, Gangadhar Rao, was a scholar in Sanskrit and grammar. He was fearless and had great self-respect – the qualities inherited by his son. Even during his school years, he was respected by his companions. He was moved by the plight of the poor and was always ready to serve them. The people considered him worthy of respect and addressed him as 'Tilak'.

Tilak tried to revive a sense of pride among Hindus for their ancient culture and traditions. Tilak's statement "Swaraj is my birthright and I shall have it" was considered anti-government. Fearless that he was, he worked undaunted for the independence of India.

Lokmanya Tilak married at the young age of 15, but after graduating, he joined the freedom struggle. For the dissemination of nationalist thoughts, he first opened a school, then he began publishing two newspapers – *Mahratta* in English and *Kesari* in

Marathi. To invoke a sense of national pride, he wrote provocative articles against the British Government. So he had to face several punishments and imprisonments. To instil a sense of unity, he organised 'Ganesh Chaturthi' and 'Shivaji Jayanti'. He celebrated and popularised these occasions as great festivals.

He spent six months' rigorous imprisonment in Mandalay Jail, Burma due to his alleged support for the murder of a British couple. The more the punishment imposed on him, the more his fame grew and the more people revered him. The British tried to stop the publication of his newspapers.

Lokmanya Tilak was a scholar of Sanskrit, Mathematics, Astrology, History and Philosophy. He was also a great writer. Among the significant books he wrote, were *The Secret of the Gita, Orion, The True Home of the Aryans* and others. *The Secret of the Gita* is an annotation of the Holy *Gita* which believes that work is worship.

Lokmanya Tilak was the symbol of Indianness. The youth respected him. The public had profound reverence for him. On his death, Gandhiji remarked, "The public considers Lokmanya Tilak as a god and his words as words from the *Vedas*."

In 1920, he was chosen the president of the Congress, but he died in July before the session. Lokmanya Tilak was one of the greatest nationalist leaders whom his countrymen can never forget.

Madan Mohan Malaviya

The Epitome of Indian Culture

(1861–1946)

A mong the prominent personalities of the 20th Century, there was one person who could be called India's foremost monk. And the speciality of this monk was that he got donations in lakhs, but never spent a penny of the donations on himself.

Malaviyaji had pledged that the modern education system be modified and developed to suit the Indian context. And so he established the Benares Hindu University. He collected donations from kings, princes, financers and industrialists for the purpose. Malaviyaji commanded a lot of respect and so, nobody could give him less than a few lakhs. Malaviyaji's efforts to save Hindu culture, thereby contributing to the rejuvenation of Indian culture, made him one of the prominent Indians of the 20th Century.

Malaviyaji also tried to foil the growing influence and coercion of Christianity and Islam. Just as Ashutosh Mukherjee strived for the propagation of education and science in Bengal, Malaviyaji tried to safeguard Indian culture by establishing the Hindu University. The University had the pride of having Dr S. Radhakrishnan as one of its Vice-Chancellors.

Malaviyaji was an Indian to the core through his mind, body and dress code. He was always dressed in homespun cloth. He wore a long white *angrakha*, a *tilak* on his forehead and a white Khaddar or homespun cloth as a turban. All his life he tried to safeguard Indian culture from the influence of the West.

He was born on 25 December 1861 at Allahabad in a *Karamkandi* Brahmin family. His father Brijnath Malaviya was a Sanskrit scholar and devoted most of his time to virtuous predisposition. After completing his education, Malaviyaji was compelled to take up teaching as a profession, though his desire was to take up politics. Even while in school, he was fond of writing poems and plays. He wrote under the pseudonym 'Makrand'. He considered poet Bharatendu as his guru. He devoted his whole life to teaching and his greatest achievement was the Benares Hindu University. The University has a memorial in recognition of his contribution.

Malaviyaji also excelled as a journalist. Apart from *Hindustan*, the King of Kalankar, Rampal Singh brought out *Leader* and *The Hindustan Times* with the help of Malaviyaji. Then Malaviyaji left the editorial work of *Hindustan* and studied law. He went on to become one of the distinguished lawyers of Allahabad. He gave up his practice in 1911, but took up the case of the accused in the infamous Chauri Chaura incident of 1922 and got them acquitted before the Allahabad High Court. He was chosen the president of the Congress at the Lahore Congress Session held in 1909. He went to jail several times in connection with the freedom struggle. He died on 12 November 1946.

In spite of being an eminent scholar and a prominent leader, he never gave up the Indian way of dressing and culture. He was the epitome of Indian culture.

Maulana Abul Kalam Azad

Theologian and Prominent Leader

(1888–1958)

Maulana Azad was born in Mecca, Saudi Arabia, to an eminent Indian scholar and an Arab mother. He was brought up and educated strictly along Islamic lines in Calcutta, but he secretly learned English. However, in spite of his firm belief in Islam, he did not accept the partition of India on religious grounds. Maulana Azad worked towards the solidarity of the nation and was never influenced by religious fundamentalism.

Not many people are aware of the contribution he made towards the freedom struggle. Maulana Azad never came to the limelight and let Gandhiji and Pt Nehru take all the credit. He even formed the Nationalist Muslim Party within the Congress to disprove the claim of the Muslim League that it represented all Muslims. Pt Jawaharlal Nehru considered Azad a symbol of courage and culture.

Maulana Azad founded the University Grants Commission. His contribution towards psychological study and technical education is also immense. He also founded the All India Council for Technical Education.

On the one hand, he showed an interest in adult literacy, female literacy, scientific and technical education and higher education; on the other, he also worked for the acknowledgement of arts, music and literature at the national level. He founded the Sahitya Akademi, the Sangeet Natak Akademi and the Lalit Kala Akademi with much zeal. Sahitya Akademi is a national organisation and promotes literature in all the prominent languages of India by giving awards to the best writers in regional languages. When the Sahitya Akademi was founded, it did not have a building. Maulana Azad gave a portion of his house to set up an office of the Akademi. In his 10-year stint as education minister, Maulana Azad contributed a lot for the promotion of education, art and literature.

Maulana Azad was a recipient of many literary awards. He also translated the Koran. Maulana Azad had a firm belief in Islam. His life is an example of the impact religion makes on a true follower. Pt Nehru said that Azad was an ideal religious person.

He said the following words to the people affected by the communal riots immediately after Partition.

Chalo Aao Tumhe Dikhayein
Jo Bacha Hai Mahatal-e-Shehar Mein
Ahal-e-Sidak Ki Turbatein

(Come, I'll show you what is left of the town of executioners. Here lie the graves of true, honest and religious men.)

Maulana Azad was known for his integrity. In his book, *India Wins Freedom*, he blames both the Congress leaders and Mohammad Ali Jinnah for the partition of the country. He was strongly opposed to partition.

He passed away on 22 February 1958. He was posthumously awarded India's highest civilian award, the Bharat Ratna in 1992.

Veer Savarkar

Revolutionary Hindu Activist

(1883-1966)

Vinayak Damodar Savarkar is better remembered as Veer Savarkar because he faced the atrocities of the British Raj with great fortitude. When he was exiled to the Andamans, he was yoked to the milling machine and made to extract 30 pounds of mustard oil by crushing. The young lad was very brave, but the atrocities damaged his health and he could never lead a healthy life. And when the *Hindi-Chini Bhai-Bhai* chanting Chinese attacked India, he was shocked. On 26 February 1966, he fell unconscious and died subsequently.

Veer Savarkar was born on 28 May 1883 at Nasik in Maharashtra. He was fondly called Tatya. He had two brothers. Their parents narrated them stories from the *Ramayana* and the *Mahabharata* and also the adventurous tales of Shivaji and Maharana Pratap. So the feeling of patriotism was instilled in Savarkar right from childhood. Maharashtra had produced another valiant hero, Lokmanya Tilak. When Veer Savarkar met Tilak, his spirit of nationalism became stronger.

The effect of the influence was that whenever a couple or more boys met, they discussed patriotism. Even in his school, he constituted a group called 'Mitramandali'. Gradually his influence increased and people praised him.

After completing his BA, he wanted to study law. So he went to London. But he met a few Indian revolutionaries there who made plans against the British Empire and gave them shape. The chief revolutionaries were Shyamji Krishna Verma and Madanlal Dhingra. Savarkar stayed at India House in London, which had by then become the centre of Indian revolutionary activities. Savarkar, who was already a patriot, now began to participate in the activities of the revolutionaries with more vigour. So the British Government sent him back to India. But he jumped off the ship that was carrying him back to India because he wanted to be a free man. However, the officials caught him and transported him to the Andamans. His brother Ganesh Savarkar was also undergoing imprisonment in the same jail. Savarkar stayed there for 10 years. After he was released, he was kept under house arrest in Ratnagiri. It was here that he met Subhash Chandra Bose.

Behind the thin, frail body was the strong, resonating mind of a Hindu activist. He also wanted to develop the feeling of Hindu activism as a strong force. And towards this end, he founded the Hindu Mahasabha. He invoked the feeling of self-pride among Hindus. In 1948, he was arrested for alleged involvement in the assassination of Mahatma Gandhi, but the court did not find him guilty of any conspiracy. Savarkar did not have any malice towards anyone. His acts of patriotism and the sufferings he faced on the path of national struggle are proof enough that he was totally committed to the cause of nationalism.

He considered the Hindu Mahasabha as the Hindu National Mahasabha. The Hindu Mahasabha participated in a number of elections, but in a country that was influenced by the views of Mahatma Gandhi, it failed to achieve success.

Veer Savarkar was also a good writer. His work *The First War of National Independence* is considered very significant.

Aruna Asaf Ali

An Icon of Courage

(1909–1996)

The courageous and defiant Aruna Asaf Ali finds a place of honour in India's independence struggle and socialist revolution. Initially she was associated with the Congress and in 1948, after Independence, she joined the Socialist Party of Acharya Narendra Dev. Later she joined the Communist Party and remained associated with the party till the end through the presidentship of their *Patriot* group of newspapers.

Aruna Asaf Ali gained instant fame and recognition for the valour she displayed in 1942 during the Quit India Movement when she broke the police barricade and hoisted the Congress flag at Oval Maidan in Bombay. This was a task well achieved for a 30-year-old lady. She went into hiding after the incident and resurfaced in 1946, after the new government formed by the Congress withdrew the arrest warrant issued against her. The secret service of the British Government had announced a reward of Rs 5,000 – a big amount in those days – for anyone who could provide clues about her whereabouts. Her property and wealth were impounded too. Yet she could not be caught. Although she went into hiding, she did not remain inactive. She toured the country and instilled a feeling of nationalism among the masses.

Aruna was born into a Bengali family on 16 July 1909 in Kalka (Haryana). Her father was a doctor, but he died when she was too young. Her mother sent her to Nainital for studies, where she came in contact with the Nehru family. This association instilled political awareness in her. After returning from Nainital, she joined a school in Calcutta. On one occasion, when she went to Allahabad to meet her sister, she met a well-known Muslim lawyer Asaf Ali. The meeting soon blossomed into love and they got married. Both participated in the activities of the Congress together. In 1930, she was imprisoned at Lahore for a year for her participation in the satyagraha movement. Again in 1932, she was jailed for six months. These sentences made her stronger from within and helped her carry out the courageous feat of 1942.

After Independence, she settled in Delhi and dedicated herself to social service. She was also elected the Mayor of Delhi in 1958. She published a magazine, *Link* and established 'Saraswati Bhavan' – an institution that was concerned with education and service to the poor and underprivileged.

In 1992, she was awarded the Jawaharlal Nehru Award for International Understanding. In recognition of her services, the government conferred the Bharat Ratna on her posthumously in 1997.

Aruna Asaf Ali left for her heavenly abode on 29 July 1996.

Lala Lajpat Rai

Punjab Kesari

(1865–1928)

In the 20th Century, there have been many fearless national leaders who never hesitated in taking up challenges. Netaji Subhash Chandra Bose is an illustrious example of such a leader. And there was another – Punjab Kesari Lala Lajpat Rai. He was loved and respected not only in India, but also in America. His life is a tale of supreme sacrifice. In spite of coming from a well-to-do family, he chose to serve the nation. He protested against the Simon Commission before Bredma Hall in Lahore and took the brunt of the lathi charge over his head. And this led to his untimely demise.

He hailed from Punjab and always spoke in chaste Punjabi. His khaddar turban was his identity. He toured the world, but never gave up his identity and his pride of being an Indian.

His fearlessness and sense of social service earned him the title of Punjab Kesari. Lala Lajpat Rai was born on 28 January 1865 into an Agarwal family in a small village named Jagraon in Moga district of Punjab. After his formal education, he went to Lahore to study. He practised at Lahore and Hisar. At Lahore, he helped establish the nationalist Anglo-Vedic School and became a follower of Swami Dayanand, the founder of the Arya Samaj. Slowly his area of work expanded. He travelled across the nation and helped people suffering from famine.

At 23, he joined the Congress. It was because of his zealous efforts that the Congress Session at Lahore in 1893 became a success. The British Government saw the makings of a revolutionary in Lalaji and exiled him to Mandalay Jail in Burma (now Myanmar) in May 1907 without any trial. However because of lack of sufficient evidence, he was allowed to return in November the same year.

In December 1907 the supporters of Lalaji wanted to elect him the president of the Congress, but leaders who believed in seeking favours from the British refused to accept him. Because of differences, the party split.

Lala Lajpat Rai realised that there was a lack of nationalism among the youth of Punjab. So he established the Lok Sevak Sangh to provide financial assistance to those youths who were engaged in the service of the nation. During the Second World War, he went to the United States. He returned in1919. In 1920, he led the special session of the Congress that launched the Non-cooperation Movement. Between 1921 and 1923, he was put in prison. On his release he was elected to the Legislative Assembly.

In 1928, he introduced the Legislative Assembly resolution for the boycott of the Simon Commission. When the Simon Commission came to India, it was boycotted by the whole nation. In Lahore, Lalaji led a protest march against the Commission. The peace marchers were mercilessly lathi-charged. Lalaji received a blow on his head and was badly injured. A few days later, on 17 November 1928 he succumbed to his injuries. Later, revolutionaries killed Superintendent Saunders, the police officer who was responsible for Lalaji's death.

In the Congress, the triad of Lal (Lala Lajpat Rai), Bal (Bal Gangadhar Tilak) and Pal (Bipin Chandra Pal) were very famous.

Lala Lajpat Rai wrote a number of books. Some of the prominent ones include *The Story of My Deportation* (1908), *Arya Samaj* (1915), *The United States of America: A Hindu's Impression* (1916) and *Unhappy India* (1928).

C. Rajagopalachari

First Governor-General of India

(1878–1972)

Chakravarti Rajagopalachari, better known as Rajaji, was a freedom fighter, statesman, scholar, thinker, humorist and humanist. Along with Gandhi, Nehru and Patel, he was one of the strong pillars of the Indian National Congress. After Independence he succeeded Lord Mountbatten as the Governor-General of India.

Born on 10 December 1878 at Thorapalli village in Hosur taluka of Salem district to Chakravarti Iyengar and Singaramma, C. Rajagopalachari graduated from the Presidency College, Madras. He received his Bachelor of Law degree in 1899. After this, he started practice in Salem in 1900, and soon reached the peak of glory in his profession. He won practically all his cases. Rajaji had met Gandhiji in 1919 and like the latter he was upset by the Rowlatt Committee recommendations. Later he became Gandhiji's lieutenant in the south. During the freedom struggle, Rajaji was jailed several times.

Rajaji also organised a successful Flag Satyagraha in Nagpur in 1923. Like Gandhiji he too transgressed the Salt Act on 13 April 1930, by leading a 150-mile march of 98 satyagrahis from Trichy to Vedarnyam. Rajaji played a leading part in shaping the Poona Pact. He had the unique ability of resolving differences between Hindus and Muslims and for that reason he was made the Governor of Bengal in 1947.

Later when the term of Lord Mountbatten ended, Rajaji was made the first Governor-General of India. He was awarded the Bharat Ratna in 1954.

Rajaji passed away on 25 December 1972.

Lal Bahadur Shastri

Leader of Towering Integrity

(1904–1966)

Although Lal Bahadur Shastri was just five feet in height and had a thin physique, he was a leader of towering integrity. Shastriji became the Prime Minister of India after the death of Pt Nehru. This surprised many, as Shastriji came from a humble background. But he rose to the position of prime minister solely on merit and it was because of these qualities that Pt Nehru had faith in his competence.

His competence was proved immediately after he took over as prime minister. At that time Pakistan was ruled by the dictator Marshal Ayub Khan. Pt Nehru's death was hastened because, in 1962, China invaded India in spite of our cordial relations. Panchsheel and *Hindi-Chini Bhai-Bhai* failed miserably. This was a shock for Pt Nehru and he could not recover from it. After Shastriji took over as the prime minister, he showed tremendous courage and was not deterred by the threats of Ayub Khan. Shastriji said that if Pakistan had its eyes on Delhi, we will protect it, and will gallantly reach Lahore. Shastriji won great popularity for the firmness with which he handled the issue of Kashmir.

In the war that ensued, the Indian Army took large parts of Pakistan. The army laid siege to Lahore, which was within firing range of army tanks. It was at this juncture that the now defunct Soviet Union intervened. Both the leaders went to Tashkent for negotiations. On the advice of the USSR, India agreed to hand over all the captured areas back to Pakistan. After he signed the Tashkent Agreement with President Ayub Khan, Indian forces withdrew from Pakistan. Perhaps Shastriji thought that people back home would not like his decision. He went to sleep with a heavy heart. He suffered a heart attack at night and died in his sleep.

Shastriji was born into a Kayastha family on 2 October 1904 in the town of Mughalsarai, Uttar Pradesh. In the initial stages of his life, he suffered many hardships. His father, Sharda Prasad Srivastava, was a teacher. Shastriji's father died when he was just an infant. So his mother Ramdulari Devi took him to her father's home. As he had a small frame even as a child, he was called *Nanhe*.

Some accounts state that Shastriji used to swim across the Ganges to reach school because he did not have the money to pay the boatman who ferried people across the river. After completing his fifth standard, he was sent to his uncle Raghunath's house in Varanasi where he was admitted to Harishchandra High School. Because of his pleasing manners and interest in studies, he soon became a favourite among his teachers. It was during these days that Bal Gangadhar Tilak, the nationalist leader, paid a visit to Varanasi. His words left an indelible impact on young Shastriji's mind. Inspired by Tilak and the Non-cooperation Movement, he left school although he was required to sit through just another month to complete high school.

On one occasion, he participated in a protest rally during the Non-cooperation Movement. Though he was around 16 at that time, he seemed a young boy of around 12–13 because of his short stature and frail frame. The police arrested him along with the other protestors, but let him go after questioning because they mistook him to be a boy.

It was during those days that Madan Mohan Malaviya established the Kashi Vidyapeeth (now Mahatma Gandhi Kashi Vidyapeeth). Shastriji sought admission in the institute and obtained the title of *Shastri* (learned in the Scriptures).

After completing his education, he sought a source of livelihood. Lala Lajpat Rai had just established the Lok Seva Mandal. Inspired by Lalaji's ideals, Shastriji became a life member of the institution and dedicated himself to the service of the people. The institution provided its members a monthly stipend but that could barely fulfil the basic needs of a family. Shastriji was married to Lalita Devi when he was just 17. It was because of his wife's whole-hearted cooperation that it became easier for Shastriji to work for the freedom struggle. It is said that Shastriji accepted just a spinning wheel and handspun khadi cloth as dowry.

As part of his work at the Lok Sevak Mandal, he used to visit Allahabad and there he came in contact with Pt Nehru. He was appointed the general secretary of the Allahabad Congress Committee. Between 1930 and 1945, he participated in a number of movements and spent almost nine years in prison.

In 1942, when Gandhiji gave the call for 'Quit India', he was arrested along with other prominent leaders in Bombay. He, however, escaped and reached Allahabad. He held the belief that before embarking on a new venture, one should take the blessings of one's mother. He reached home at four o'clock in the morning and took his mother's blessings. Exactly at five, he went to Allahabad Square and addressed thousands of people gathered there. Here the police arrested him.

In 1937 and 1946, Shastriji was elected to the Legislature of the United Provinces. After Independence, he served as Minister of Home Affairs and Transportation in the Uttar Pradesh Government. In 1952, Shastriji was elected to the Central Legislature. Pt Nehru later appointed him as the Railway Minister in the Central Cabinet. But in August 1956, when a terrible rail mishap occurred near Mehboob Nagar, he resigned owning moral responsibility. Such instances of humility made him a highly respected personality.

In 1961, he was appointed the Minister for Home Affairs. In early 1964, when Pt Nehru took ill, he was appointed Minister without Portfolio and later, in June 1964, he became the prime minister after Pt Nehru's death.

Shastriji was posthumously honoured with the Bharat Ratna in 1966.

Dadabhai Naoroji

Founder-Member of the INC

(1825–1917)

Dadabhai Naoroji is one of those personalities who were respected by the British and also honoured by Indians. He was considered to be a father-figure among nationalists, being a founder-member of the Indian National Congress (INC). Dadabhai not only worked towards attaining independence but also inspired many educated people to join hands with him.

Dadabhai Naoroji was born on 4 September 1825 in a Parsi family. In 1845, he did his B.A. and ten years later went to London. There, he assisted Bhikhaji Cama, a leading businessman, in his business. He organised the Indians living in London and formed the Indian Society. After some time he was chosen to be a member of the British Parliament. One of the first Indians to have the honour of becoming a member of the British Parliament, he was known as "The Grand Old Man of India".

When Dadabhai joined the Congress, it was basically a society of government servants and its main function was to apprise the British Government about the people's problems. Dadabhai was extremely popular and was elected as its president in 1896 and 1906. Dadabhai was not satisfied with merely forwarding complaints to the government. He sought independence. He was summoned to court for his activities.

Dadabhai Naoroji is among those leaders who did not overlook the importance of keeping in touch with the British while demanding independence. He is also acclaimed as the "Father of Indian Politics and Economics".

Dadabhai Naoroji passed away on 30 June 1917 at Versova at the age of 91.

Gopal Krishna Gokhale

The Gem of Maharashtra

(1866–1915)

He has been aptly called by Lokmanya Tilak, his lifelong rival, "The diamond of India, the gem of Maharashtra." Gokhale was born on 9 May 1866 at Kotluk in Ratnagiri district in the Kolhapur State of Bombay Presidency. He came from a poor Brahmin family. In 1884, he graduated from Elphinstone College, Bombay. Gokhale's brother wanted him to go to England and compete for the ICS, but he chose the humbler profession of teaching. Later he came under the influence of Justice Ranade, and under his expert guidance studied Indian Economics.

In 1900, he was elected a member of the Bombay Legislative Council, where he worked along with Sir Pherozeshah Mehta. In 1902, he was nominated to the Viceroy's Council, where his budget speeches were well known for financial criticism.

He was elected the president of the National Congress at Benares in 1905. His presidential speech is considered one of the best ever delivered on the Congress platform. Gokhale was a champion of the interests of Indians abroad. He supported their agitation in South Africa against the humiliating restraints imposed upon them. This interest in the South African problem brought him into close contact with Gandhi. He supported Gandhi's passive resistance campaign.

He played a significant role in India's freedom movement. For years he stood forth, in the eyes of both the Indian Government and the British, as the most representative Indian. He never merely criticised the government when he dealt with its shortcomings, as some of his contemporaries did. He was, in a larger sense, a reconciler between Western and Eastern culture. Gandhi affirmed Gokhale as his political guru. He died on 19 February 1915.

Chandra Shekhar Azad

The Undaunted Revolutionary

(1905–1931)

Chandra Shekhar Azad will always remain immortal in the annals of history as a man who sacrificed his life at the altar of freedom. At a time when Gandhiji was busy with his *ahimsa* and Non-cooperation Movement to liberate the country, a couple of fiery young men were sceptical about his methods. They were sure the best course was the proverbial policy of 'tit for tat' and were in favour of giving the British a fitting reply for their tyranny. Bhagat Singh, Sukhdev, Sachindra Sanyal and Ram Prasad Bismil were among those who had no faith in non-violence. While Bhagat Singh was active in Punjab, Chandra Shekhar Azad was busy in UP. He was fired by the zeal to help Bhagat Singh and when the two collaborated, Chandra Shekhar Azad was given the leadership of the activists.

Azad became a member of the group which had vowed to avenge the death of Lala Lajpat Rai. British police officer Saunders was their target. The group looted the government treasury for funds required for the movement. A terror to the police, Azad was listed a terrorist and kept under watch. He was surrounded on 27 February 1931 in Alfred Park, Allahabad, by a strong police squadron Azad fought them bravely for many hours. Even after he was killed, the British dared not approach his body and waited for some time to confirm his death.

Azad was born on 23 July 1906 at Jhabra in Madhya Pradesh. He ran away from home when young, reached Kashi (Benares) and joined the freedom struggle. In 1921, he was first sentenced to 15 lashes for revolutionary activities. With each stroke of the whip the young patriot shouted *Bharat Mata ki Jai and confounded the officers with his undaunted spirit.*

Political Leaders

Indira Gandhi

India's First Woman Prime Minister

(1917–1984)

Indira Gandhi is one of those leaders who is known more for the wrong reasons. But the sheer grit and determination she displayed by siding with the Shanti Vahini Army and helping in the formation of Bangladesh is laudable.

Indira Priyadarshini Gandhi, the only child of Jawaharlal and Kamala Nehru, was born on 19 November 1917 in Allahabad. Pt Nehru was the first Prime Minister of India. But the beliefs and works of father and daughter make it clear that the thoughts and inclinations of both were totally different. The Congress was divided when she was the president of the party and she was often accused of manipulation to keep power in her own hands, but such was not the case with Pt Nehru. There is no denying the fact that Indira was a true patriot like her father, but never in her childhood or her youth did she ever give an indication that she would transform into such a steadfast personality.

There were many ups and downs during her prime ministerial days. She remained the Prime Minister of India for almost 17 years. And to govern a vast country like India which had varied cultures, languages and customs, was definitely a challenge and Indira faced it with immense courage. And by doing so, she changed the image of India in the South Asian scenario.

After the partition of the country in 1947, Pakistan was divided into two – East and West. And having a Pakistan-administered state on either side of India was creating a problem. In the 1971 war with Pakistan, she helped East Pakistan severe ties with West Pakistan and created an independent state of Bangladesh. In doing so, she displayed tremendous determination and diplomacy.

But she also received a lot of flak for her other activities, especially for declaring Emergency in the country in 1975, at a time when the situation was not at all grim. The reason for declaring an Emergency was that the Congress was losing hold of power in the country and Indira Gandhi wanted to make sure that her position as the prime minister remained unchallenged. A number of important leaders and journalists were arrested. Freedom of the Press was curbed.

When she was young, most people called her a 'dumb doll'. It would have been nobody's guess that this 'dumb doll' would go on to become a powerful figure.

Indira's life can be broadly divided into three phases. First – her childhood, where she was forced to play with toys, dolls, and tin soldiers because her mother Kamala Nehru always remained ill and her father Pt Nehru mostly spent his life in jail. Inspired by the freedom struggle and seeing freedom fighters at close quarters when they came to discuss political strategies with her father and grandfather Motilal Nehru, she formed the 'monkey brigade'.

The second phase of her life began when she was in England. Her mother was then taken to Switzerland for treatment. It was here that she met Feroze Gandhi. It is believed that driven by emotions, she married him in haste and repented later. For most of their married life, they lived separately. After Partition and Independence, when Pt Nehru became the prime minister, she lived with her father to look after him. Kamala Nehru had died and there was no one to look after her father. Feroze and Indira had two sons, but her marital life was not happy.

The third phase of her life began in 1955 when she became an active member of the Indian National Congress. In 1959 she was elected to the post of party president, which was largely an honorary post. After Pt Nehru died, Lal Bahadur Shastri became the Prime Minister of India and included her in the Cabinet as Information & Broadcasting Minister. In 1966 she became the Prime Minister after Shastriji's sudden demise. This period was completely different from the other two phases of her life. It was during this period that she proved Shakespeare's statement, "Frailty, thy name is woman", wrong.

She took a few steps that prove that besides being fearless, she was a great patriot. She nationalised all banks. She also discontinued the privy purses that were being paid to all those kings who had agreed to join the Indian Union after Independence in exchange for the privy purses. In doing so, she ended their hold on their ancestral land and property.

But her leadership was under constant challenge from Morarji Desai. In the elections of 1967, the Congress won by a slender margin, so she had to accept Desai as the deputy prime minister. But in the elections of 1971, she was able to win by a huge margin. She supported the cause of East Bengal (now Bangladesh) in its secessionist conflict with Pakistan in 1971. The Indian Army was able to win a decisive victory over Pakistan and helped in the creation of Bangladesh. This was carried out in spite of America's protest. This act of hers was a challenge to those western forces who believed that South Asia was a region where they could carry out their selfish motives.

In the national elections held in March 1972, the Congress registered a landslide victory. But her opponents accused her of violating electoral laws and in June 1975, the High Court of Allahabad ruled against her. She was to be deprived of her seat in Parliament and debarred from active politics for six years. It was then that she declared Emergency in the country. She assumed emergency powers and most of her political opponents were imprisoned. There were curbs on personal freedom. Many harsh policies were implemented, which made the party unpopular during the time.

When the long postponed elections were finally held in 1977, the Congress party was routed. The Janata Party took over after Indira Gandhi left office following the defeat of her party.

In 1931, she attended the Congress Session for the first time with her father. In 1938, she became a member of the Congress and participated in the freedom struggle. In 1947, when Pt Nehru became the prime minister, she accompanied him on tours across the nation and helped him in carrying out his duties.

To curb the growing violence in Punjab, she carried out Operation Bluestar, which was an example of great fortitude. But as a result, Punjab was plunged into terrorist violence for almost 10 years.

After her defeat in '77, she campaigned with much fanfare. The Janata Party came to power in '77, but did not deliver as per the expectations of the electorate. So the people voted her back to power in the 1980 elections. In October 1984, she was assassinated by her own Sikh security guards in retaliation for Operation Bluestar.

Taking a retrospective of Indira's life, it is clear that she was never afraid of difficulties. She faced every problem with courage and fortitude.

Shyama Prasad Mukherjee

Founder of Jan Sangh

(1901–1953)

The 20th Century brought a number of opportunities for India, but also a tragedy. And that was the partition of the country on a communal basis, mainly due to the British Government's inclination towards the Muslim community. Gandhiji was not in favour of partition and was willing to give all possible help to the Muslims. As matters worsened, Muslims got all the sympathy and Hindus began to be called communal. During the early days, Jammu & Kashmir was ruled by Sheikh Abdullah. He had the same powers as the Prime Minister of India and the state even had its own flag. The leader of the Citizen's Council Pt Premnath Dogra and other Hindus wanted to hoist the national flag. However, their requests were turned down by Sheikh Abdullah at the instance of Pt Nehru. When Dr Shyama Prasad Mukherjee went to Jammu to resolve the issue, he was arrested. He died in a jail in Kashmir.

When Hindus settled in East and West Pakistan were being brutally killed and looted, the Congress, because of its soft-spoken nature, could neither speak against it nor do anything to mitigate the sufferings of the troubled people. It was then that Dr Shyama Prasad Mukherjee stood up and informed the Congress about the atrocities being committed on Hindus and asked the Congress to take steps for the safe passage of Hindus. He was the commerce minister in the first ministry constituted on 15 August 1947. He laid the foundation of the aeroplane-manufacturing unit Hindustan Aeronautics Ltd. in Bangalore, Chittaranjan Rail Factory, fertiliser plant etc. But in 1950, he resigned from the post in protest against the atrocities being committed on Hindus in Pakistan. And from then on he worked for the protection of the rights of Hindus till his death. It was towards this end that he went to Jammu & Kashmir where he was placed under arrest in Kathua and denied all facilities. Even his son was denied permission to see him and he died on 24 June 1953.

Shyama Prasad Mukherjee's father, Sir Ashutosh Mukherjee, was a prominent personality of Bengal. When Shyama Prasad was born, Sir Ashutosh was the lifeline of Calcutta University. After completing his education, Shyama Prasad followed the footsteps of his father and joined public service. In 1934, he became the Vice-Chancellor of Calcutta University. In 1936, he was chosen from the University area as a member of the Bengal State Assembly. In 1941 Fazlul Haque constituted a Cabinet along with the Hindus and made Shyama Prasad Mukherjee the finance minister.

In 1942, Midnapur district of Bengal came under the grip of severe floods and there was heavy loss of life and property. But the British governor denied Shyama Prasad Mukherjee permission to tour the affected areas. So he resigned from the Cabinet. Then he mobilised support and took the help of the Mahabodhi Society, the Ramakrishna Mission and the Marwari Relief Society to organise relief for those affected by the floods. It was during those days that Dhaka became the centre of riots. Dr Mukherjee held talks with the Nawab of Dhaka and helped restore peace and normalcy. Dr Mukherjee was moved to see the plight of Hindu refugees who had come from Pakistan.

Dr Mukherjee was the president of the Mahabodhi Society. When the mortal remains of Lord Buddha were brought to India from England, they were handed over to Dr Mukherjee. He took the relics to Burma, Cambodia, Vietnam and Bangkok. Wherever he went, he was welcomed with open arms and the relics were worshipped. On his return to India, he placed the relics inside the Sanchi Stupa.

In 1951, along with leaders of the Rashtriya Swayamsevak Sangh (RSS), Dr Mukherjee founded the Bharatiya Jan Sangh (BJS). Even after his death the party continued to grow stronger and gave national leaders of the stature of Atal Behari Vajpayee. The BJS was the forerunner of the Bharatiya Janata Party (BJP).

Atal Behari Vajpayee

Former Prime Minister and Veteran Parliamentarian

(Born 1924)

The name Atal Behari Vajpayee evokes such warm feelings that every Indian holds him in high esteem. Whatever he does, he always upholds the nation's pride, honour and dignity.

Atal Behari Vajpayee was born into a Brahmin family on 25 December 1924, at Gwalior, Madhya Pradesh. His father was a school teacher. Vajpayee was educated at Gwalior and Kanpur. He was a student of political science – a subject that was to prepare him for the future. Atal Behari Vajpayee was inclined towards politics even as a teenager. He was imprisoned for a brief period during the British rule for his anti-British activities. As a youth, he was attracted towards communism, but because the communists supported the partition of the country and the creation of Pakistan, he was disillusioned. It was then that he was influenced by the Rashtriya Swayamsevak Sangh (RSS), an organisation that was formed to instil a sense of honour among Hindus. He gave up his studies and joined as an editor of a publication of the RSS. In 1957, he joined the Bharatiya Jan Sangh (BJS), a forerunner of the Bharatiya Janata Party (BJP), which he was to co-found later with other political stalwarts.

Atal Behari Vajpayee was first elected to the Lok Sabha in 1957. Since then he has been elected to the Lok Sabha seven times and twice to the Rajya Sabha. During the Emergency, he was jailed along with other prominent opposition leaders. In the Janata-led Government that was elected to power in 1977, he served as foreign minister and helped strengthen ties with China and Pakistan. In 1980, he became a co-founder of the Bharatiya Janata Party (BJP) which advocates Hindutva, the feeling of pride in Hindu culture and values. Its popularity can be judged by the fact that in the 1984 elections, the party won just two seats and in the 1991 elections, it arnered so much support that it won 117 seats in the Lok Sabha. The demolition of the Babri Masjid at Ayodhya in December 1992 by organisations associated with the party led to a major setback in the party's popularity. But Atal Behari Vajpayee was one of those few leaders who regretted the demolition and condemned the act.

In May 1996, Atal Behari Vajpayee was sworn in as the eleventh prime minister. But his term lasted only 13 days because he was not able to garner enough support from other parties. In the next parliamentary elections held in 1998, the BJP and its allies formed the government led by Atal Behari Vajpayee. However the All India Anna Dravida Munnetra Kazagham (AIADMK) withdrew its support to the BJP-led Government, leading to its fall. In this brief span, India conducted the Pokhran II tests in May 1998, as Vajpayee put it 'to serve as a deterrent against our neighbours', who were harbouring evil intentions against India. The whole operation was carried out under cover and even took the Americans by surprise. There was condemnation in the West and economic sanctions were imposed on India by the US, the UK, France and other Western countries. Vajpayee remained defiant and declared: "India had the sanction of her own past glory and future vision to become strong."

As no other party had enough support to stake a claim to form the government, the country went into yet another mid-term poll in 1999. This time the BJP formed an alliance called the National Democratic Alliance (NDA), which was a coalition of different national and regional parties. The alliance won and as the leader of the largest party in the alliance, Atal Behari Vajpayee became the prime minister for the third time. He is the second prime minister after Pt Jawaharlal Nehru to be sworn in thrice.

Atal Behari Vajpayee is not just a politician, he has written several books. His speeches made as minister of external affairs have been compiled as *New Dimensions of Foreign Policy*. He is also a well-known poet. Among his published poems is *Meri Ikkyavan Kavitayen* ("My Fifty-one Poems"). The NDA got a debacle in the Lok Sabha elections held in 2004.

Dr Zakir Hussain

**Founder of Basic Education/
Former President of India**

(1897–1969)

The inspiration behind Dr Zakir Hussain's dream of basic education was Gandhiji. The deep sense of respect and love that he had for Gandhiji can be judged by the following words he said soon after being elected the president:

> *"By choosing me the President, the country has honoured a teacher. About 47 years ago, I had pledged that I would dedicate a majority of my years to national education. I had started my social life under the guidance of Gandhiji. He inspired me and showed me the way. I have now been given a new chance to serve. I will strive to lead my people through the path shown by Gandhiji."*

Dr Zakir Hussain was born on 8 February 1897 in Hyderabad. He took over as the President of India in 1967 after Dr S. Radhakrishnan. His appointment as the president reiterated that India is a secular country.

Dr Hussain was a teacher by profession. In 1937, when popular governments came up in the states, Gandhiji wanted that these governments should try to improve the level of education of their citizens. He wanted that children be given an education that would help in their mental and physical growth. Gandhiji was against the idea that education should be restricted within the school syllabus. He wanted the children to get educated through practical lessons rather than theory. This is what he called fundamental education. So he formed a committee. The work of the committee was to formulate a syllabus for basic education.

Dr Hussain made the report with great dedication. The report received lavish praise. This report was different from conventional ones. Gandhiji also liked the report and supported Dr Hussain. He was impressed by Dr Hussain's capability. So Gandhiji

59

formed the Hindustani Talimi Sangh (National Committee on Basic Education) in 1937 that was to work on the lines of Dr Hussain's report. Dr Hussain was appointed the chairman of the committee.

Dr Hussain was a descendant of the Afridi Pathans of Afghanistan. Some families of the tribe had migrated to India and settled in the Farrokhabad district of Uttar Pradesh. A majority of the people were soldiers and some were also landowners and farmers. One of the families of the tribe was that of Fida Hussain into which was born Zakir Hussain. Fida Hussain left for Hyderabad and started practising law. Zakir Hussain's early education took place in Hyderabad.

After the death of his parents, he went to Itawa to seek education and there he came in contact with a Sufi saint. This chance meeting evoked a sense of respect for every religion in the mind of young Hussain. After finishing matriculation, he went to Aligarh for further studies. It was when he was studying MA that Mahatma Gandhi beckoned students to leave State-supported institutions. Dr Zakir Hussain left college and laid the foundation of Jamia Millia Islamia (JMI). He worked in JMI for a few years and then went to Germany for further studies. He obtained a doctorate in economics from Berlin University.

After returning from Germany, he worked to improve the condition of JMI at the behest of Gandhiji and Pt Nehru. JMI shifted base from Aligarh to Delhi. He remained Vice-Chancellor of JMI for 22 years. During his years at Aligarh, he displayed such simplicity, austerity and economy that he did not have any peon or clerk to help him out with the office work. He carried out all the work himself because the financial condition of JMI was not good. At first he drew a salary of Rs 300 per month, but when he saw that JMI could not bear this expense, he himself made a cut in his salary and worked at Rs 150 per month. During his tenure at JMI, he displayed his sacrificial spirit and selflessness and did not let the institution become a centre of communal politics.

Whatever work Dr Hussain did, he left his indelible mark on it. In 1948, Dr Hussain became the Vice-Chancellor of Aligarh Muslim University. In 1952, he entered the Rajya Sabha. In 1957, when he was made the Governor of Bihar, he won the hearts of the people by his sympathy, wit, discipline and extrovert nature. In 1956-58 he served on the executive board of the United Nations Educational, Scientific and Cultural Organisation (UNESCO). Between 1962 and 1967, he served as the Vice President of India and the Chairman of the Rajya Sabha. He never discriminated between the ruling party or the opposition, nor did he let the ruling party take any advantage. After the fourth general elections when the presidential candidate was to be chosen, everyone believed that the obvious choice would be Dr Zakir Hussain. However, due to opposition the candidate had to be chosen through the ballot. But Dr Zakir Hussain emerged a clear winner. On 13 May 1967, he was appointed the President of India. The world, particularly Germany, welcomed his presidency.

Dr Hussain had a great sense of humour and had the knack of getting work done from his colleagues. Once a child had come to school wearing a dirty cap. He washed the cap for the child and taught the child a lesson in cleanliness. Once some windowpanes were so dirty that they could not be cleaned, so he broke them. He had a servant who had the habit of getting up late in the morning. One day, Dr Hussain threw a bucket of water over him and said, "Sir, have your bath. The water is ready. I have brought your morning tea. Do wake up or it will turn cold." From that day onwards, the servant used to always get up on time.

Dr Zakir Hussain loved flowers, different types of stones, jewellery and paintings. Dr Hussain also wrote a few books. In recognition of Zakir Hussain's contributions, he was conferred the Bharat Ratna in 1963.

Dr Zakir Hussain died on 3 May 1969, the first Indian President to die in office. He is buried on the campus of the Jamia Millia Islamia (a central University) in New Delhi.

Rajiv Gandhi

The Youngest Prime Minister of India

(1944–1991)

When Rajiv Gandhi became the Prime Minister of India, everyone said that he would not be able to hold the reigns of the government for long because he was inexperienced. But what they forgot was that he was born into the Nehru-Gandhi family, which was politically involved with the freedom struggle and later in nation building. So Rajiv Gandhi inherited the political legacy of the Nehru-Gandhi family from Pt Motilal Nehru, Pt Jawaharlal Nehru, Indira Gandhi and Feroze Gandhi. Rajiv Gandhi was young, dynamic and a man with foresight. It is only because of his sincere endeavour that the country is today a leading name in the I.T. revolution and mass communication.

Rajiv Gandhi was the youngest Prime Minister of India. In 1984, after the assassination of his mother Indira Gandhi, Rajiv Gandhi became the prime minister. His brother, Sanjay, had earlier died in a plane crash. Sanjay Gandhi was politically inclined from the start but Rajiv Gandhi was not. Rajiv Gandhi studied in a public school in Dehradun and later in England. Rajiv was trained as a pilot and joined the Indian Airlines. While in England, Rajiv met Sonia, an Italian citizen, whom he married later. Both were happy in their household when tragedy struck the Gandhi family. Sanjay Gandhi died in a plane crash in 1980. Sanjay was being groomed as Indira Gandhi's political heir. It was then that she decided to take Rajiv under her wing and groom him as her political heir. In spite of protests from Sonia, Rajiv joined the political arena and began to assist his mother.

In October 1984, Indira Gandhi was assassinated by her own security guards. Rajiv Gandhi was sworn in as the prime minister. In the general elections that followed, the Congress emerged the clear winner with a huge majority. And Rajiv Gandhi was sworn in as the prime minister. The people had high hopes from their young leader and he also won the respect and admiration of world leaders. However, on the home front, the opposition began to harp on the issue of Bofors and this resulted in his growing unpopularity. So in the 1989 elections, the Congress was defeated.

V.P. Singh was sworn in as the Prime Minister of India. He was the leader of the Janata Dal. The implementation of the Mandal Commission report during his tenure soon made him unpopular and he was forced to resign after losing a no-confidence motion. Chandra Shekhar took over, but the Janata Dal could not complete its five-year term. The 15-month-old ninth Lok Sabha was dissolved and fresh general elections were announced.

The nation's allegience shifted towards Rajiv Gandhi and the Congress. They wanted a stable government that would last its full term in office. Rajiv Gandhi went on a whirlwind tour of the nation to ensure the vote of the masses. However, on 21 May 1991, Rajiv was assassinated by a lady suicide bomber of the LTTE at Sriperumbudur in Tamil Nadu.

On 17 June 1991, he was posthumously awarded the Bharat Ratna. The Congress legacy is now being carried on by Sonia Gandhi and their charismatic son Rahul.

Dr Ram Manohar Lohia

Socialist Leader

(1910–1967)

Dr Ram Manohar Lohia's name is reckoned amongst the greatest Indian thinkers of the past Century. He was one of the first to foster the socialist ideology and work towards its cause. If we analyse his thoughts in retrospect, we will realise that he was basically advocating extremist thoughts. But this gentleman was born in an era when extremist thoughts were looked down upon.

Most Indians consider themselves god-fearing and do not think it proper to foster extremist thoughts. But Lohia believed that if we as responsible men and women did nothing for the oppressed classes, then talking about god was in vain.

On one hand, Lohia was a champion of democratic thought and a good orator on India's democratic principles. On the other, he gave it the form of a revolution and kindled its flame in the hearts of millions of Indians. Communist ideology was a part of that revolution which believed that casteism and religious fundamentalism were handicaps to the progress of a country and damaging to society. He believed that it was because of these wrong ideologies that mankind was losing its compassion. His speeches about this subject were full of passion. He had also penned down most of his thoughts. Just as he was against casteism, he also firmly opposed socialist dogmas.

He also opposed the principles of the Congress, although in the beginning he was associated with the Congress. But he soon felt that the ideology of the Congress was a hindrance to the progress of the nation. So he left the Congress and tried to steer the country towards communist ideology.

It is believed that the ancestors of Dr Ram Manohar Lohia

traded in iron and so took the name 'Lohia'. Ram Manohar was born in Ayodhya. His mother died when he was very young. His father, Hiralal Lohia, was a firm believer in the ideology of the Congress. When the Simon Commission came to India, Ram Manohar Lohia was pursuing his education at Calcutta University. He led the students of Calcutta. After completing his education, Lohia received a scholarship and went to Germany to conduct research in Economics. After his return he joined the Congress Socialist Party. For some time, he edited the party's weekly newsletter *Congress Socialist*. He actively participated in the country's freedom struggle and went to jail several times. In 1948, he resigned from the Congress and joined the Communist Party. He was chosen chief secretary of the party.

Dr Lohia was a powerful orator. His style of delivering speeches was utterly original. When he was a Member of Parliament, Pt Nehru respected his policies and ideology. Whether Dr Lohia made speeches inside the Parliament or outside, the audience would listen to him spellbound, and there would be pindrop silence in the hall. Almost all the top Congress leaders feared confrontation with him. He led an extremely simple and austere life. So people called him a "political sage".

One of the most loved leaders of the past Century's intellectual class died on 12 October 1967, but his revolutionary thinking continues to inspire people.

Jyoti Basu

Chief Minister with a Record Tenure

(1914-2010)

What made Jyoti Basu special is the fact that despite owing allegiance to the Communist Party (Marxist), he was elected democratically to become the longest reigning chief minister. He was elected to the position when he was 63 and held on to it till 86. He gave up his position only in the year 2000 due to failing health.

When the Communist Party first came to power, a majority of the people did not have any experience in running the state's affairs. But it was because of Jyoti Basu's political acumen, discernment and wisdom that he could hold on to his position by getting elected five times consecutively. His party CPI(M) had run the West Bengal Government under the leadership of B. Bhattacharya till middle of 2011 when Mamta Banerjee of Trinamool Congress took over the reigns.

The reason behind Jyoti Basu's immense popularity was that his government always cared for the cause of farmers and workers.

In the 1977 general and state elections, the Congress faced a terrible defeat in the Lok Sabha and the State Assembly elections. Even in West Bengal, the Congress was routed. The void left by the Congress in the political arena of West Bengal was filled by the Communist Party (Marxist) under the able leadership of Jyoti Basu.

Jyoti Basu studied in St. Xavier's School and Presidency College. Then he went to England to study law. There he came in contact with Harold Lasky, a renowned communist leader. Among Jyoti Basu's close associates were Rajni Patel, Mohan Kumaramangalam, Renu Chakravarti, Nikhil Chakravarti and Arun Bose.

Jyoti Basu had joined the Indian Communist Party at a time when the British Government had declared it illegal. In 1964, Jyoti Basu formed the Communist Party (Marxist). He was a member of the Central Committee and the Politburo right from the beginning. Under his successful administration the state of Bengal took great strides.

Jyoti Basu served as the Chief Minister of West Bengal from 1977 to 2000, making him the longest serving Chief Minister of any Indian State. He had remained a member of the CPI(M) Politburo from the time of party's founding in 1964 until 2008. Thereafter, until his death in 2010, he remained a permanent invitee to the Central Committee of CPI(M).

On 17 January 2010, Jyoti Basu breathed his last in a Kolkata hospital following pneumonia and multiple organ failure.

Chandrababu Naidu

The IT-savvy CM of Andhra Pradesh

(Born 1951)

Andhra Pradesh has produced many eminent people who have contributed a lot for the progress of the state, yet it is plagued by many problems. Some parts of Andhra Pradesh are backward and infested by Naxalites. Some of these problems came down to Chandrababu Naidu as a legacy, while many were created during his tenure. What is significant about Chandrababu Naidu is that he transformed the Nizam's old city into such an amazing world of Information Technology that his work finds mention not only in India, but also abroad. This was proved from the fact that the then President of America, Bill Clinton, included the city in his itinerary when he visited the country and praised Chandrababu Naidu for his work.

Apart from carrying out wonderful work in the field of Information Technology, he consolidated the position of his party, Telugu Desam, by joining hands with the National Democratic Alliance (NDA) and helping Atal Behari Vajpayee in forming a strong government at the Centre. Both at the national and the state level, he has displayed prudence and stability. He gave his full allegiance to the government, but also remained loyal to his state. It is because of this reason that he did not support those decisions of the Centre which could be harmful for his state or its people.

Chandrababu Naidu was born in a poor farmer's family in Chittoor district of Andhra Pradesh. He was inclined towards politics even in his youth, so before finishing his education, he joined the Congress. But seeing the zeal of this youth, Telugu Desam leader NT Rama Rao inducted him into his party and appointed him the general secretary. NT Rama Rao gave his daughter in marriage to Chandrababu Naidu. But after NTR's death, when his second wife Laxmi Parvati tried to usurp power, Naidu intervened and took over the reigns of the party. He became the Chief Minister of the state in September 1995.

Chandrababu Naidu has the same beliefs as Atal Behari Vajpayee over the success of a coalition government. His Telugu Desam Party played a key role in the formation of the government at the Centre. Naidu is one of the few chief ministers who has worked to put his state on the path of progress. He is also fully aware of the primary necessities of the people of his state.

Chandrababu Naidu is a man with foresight. In a very short time, he has etched his name in the list of prominent personalities of the 20th Century. He was defeated by Congress in May 2004 assembly elections.

Bidhan Chandra Roy

The Founder of Modern Bengal

(1882–1962)

Apart from the contribution of barristers and lawyers in the freedom struggle, many doctors also participated and prominent among them was Dr Bidhan Chandra Roy. Although Dr Ghosh was appointed the first Chief Minister of Bengal after Independence, the public wanted Dr Roy to occupy the position. The reason was that after Partition, Bengal suffered immensely and people believed that only Dr Roy could restore normalcy and put the state on the path to progress. When Dr Roy was appointed the chief minister, he did not spare any efforts to transform the state. He established the Durgapur Steel Factory, Chittaranjan Rail Factory and the Damodar Valley Corporation.

Dr Bidhan Chandra Roy was the descendant of King Pratapaditya, a legendary figure of Bengal. All his life Pratapaditya displayed valour and fought against the Mughals. But his army was no match against the army of Jehangir and he was captured. When he was being taken to be presented before the court of Jehangir, he killed himself rather than face disgrace.

The opulence of the family had been drained during his father's time itself, so Dr Roy had to face a lot of difficulties in his education. After completing his B.A. from Patna, he went to Calcutta to study medicine at the Medical College. Then he went to England and received the degrees of MRCP and FRCS. After that he worked in the regional health services.

While in Calcutta University, Dr Roy was closely associated with the famous leader Sir Ashutosh Mukherjee. So when the latter founded the Carmichael Medical College, he invited Dr Roy to join the institution. Dr Roy left his job and joined the college in 1919 and remained associated with it till the end.

When he became the chief minister, he did not resign from it, but took leave.

Sir Ashutosh was the inspiration behind Dr Roy's entry into politics. When the elections were held in 1923, Dr Roy stood for the first time from Calcutta (N) area. Sir Surendranath Banerjee was his opponent. Dr Roy defeated him by 3,500 votes.

Then it became difficult for him to separate himself from the Congress. In 1931, he was elected the Mayor of Calcutta. He had by then become a national leader. In the Congress Session held in Calcutta in 1926, he was elected Minister of the Committee. The satyagraha movement in Bengal was led by Dr Roy. In 1934, he was elected the president of the Bengal Congress.

West Bengal will never be able to forget the contributions of Dr Bidhan Chandra Roy. He died in July 1962 at the age of 80.

Dr Bidhan Chandra Roy was awarded Bharat Ratna in the year 1961.

Industrialists and Entrepreneurs

JRD Tata

Industrialist and Visionary

(1904–1993)

JRD Tata is considered an eminent personality and industrialist of the past Century. He belongs to India's leading family of industrialists who pioneered the country's industrial development. The acumen and foresight that he displayed led to such sustained growth of Tata Industries that one is forced to make a study of the conglomerate. When JRD Tata became the chairman of the Tata Group, it had just 15 companies. Because of his planning the Tata Group grew into 100 companies.

The Tata Group has diversified into a number of areas and is totally engrossed in the service of the people through its hospitals and other service centres.

Jehangir Ratanji Dadabhoy Tata or simply JRD Tata was born on 29 July 1904 in Paris. He was also educated in Paris. In 1938, after the death of Sir Naoroji Saklatvala, one of the nephews of the founders of the company, JRD Tata took over as the chairman of the Tata Group.

JRD Tata was the first Indian to have gained the permission and licence to fly an aeroplane. He first flew from Karachi to Bombay in 1929. There were no special provisions at airports in those days. When he flew from Karachi, the area around the airport was full of ditches. In 1930, he went on a solo flight from Bombay to England on a single-seater aeroplane. And then he founded Tata Airlines in 1932. In 1953, when the race for nationalisation was on, Tata Airlines was nationalised and split into Indian Airlines Corporation, the country's domestic air service, and Air-India, the international carrier.

After JRD took over the reins in 1938, Tata Group took huge strides. He used to trust his people a lot. And some of his most trusted men were S. Mulgaonkar who looked after TELCO, Darbari Seth of Tata Chemicals, Ajit Kerkar who looked after the Taj Group of Hotels, and Russi Modi of TISCO. These were some of the prominent personalities who steered the Tata Group of Industries to staggering heights.

JRD Tata was one of the closest associates of Pt Nehru. However, in spite of this amiable relationship between them, JRD never hesitated to convey his displeasure to Pt Nehru if he found any of the latter's plans inappropriate.

He used to say that he often had to part with people with whom he was closely associated. He knew that whoever came into this world had to depart one day. He was closely associated with the head of the Indian Nuclear Centre, Dr Homi Bhabha. JRD expressed the above thoughts when Dr Homi Bhabha died in an aircrash while returning from Vienna.

The secret of JRD's success was that he did every task with complete dexterity. And this was one of the reasons he was chosen the adviser to a number of committees formed by the government. If he felt that the decisions taken by the government or other committees were inappropriate, he would put forth his view on the subject with such conviction that the other members had no choice but to abide by his wishes.

He not only expanded the Tata empire, but did a lot for the welfare of the people. He set up some of the finest hospitals. In 1992, the government honoured him with the Bharat Ratna.

The ancestors of JRD Tata came to India from Iran when they were being forced to convert to Islam. One of his ancestors Jamshedji Nusserwanji was a man with foresight who set up a steel industry at Jamshedpur and started the industrial revolution. Today Tata Group of Industries is one of the top industrial houses of India.

JRD Tata died on 29 November 1993 in Geneva, Switzerland at the of age of 89.

Ghanshyam Das Birla

Founder of the Birla Group

(1894–1983)

Apart from being an indomitable personality in the industrial field, Ghanshyam Das Birla had many other special qualities. There has been no industrial baron in India who not only found success in his business, but also strode the field of politics with the same poise and confidence. And this was not all. Ghanshyam Das Birla initiated a number of programmes for the betterment of society. He said that earning money was not as difficult as choosing the right way to spend it. He built many temples where people could find solace and peace.

When we look at his entire life in retrospect, we come to the conclusion that he was different from other industrialists. One proof is that he started an industry at a time when the Europeans had a firm hold on Indian industries. And he started some other industries which no one had thought of before.

Ghanshyam Das Birla had an elementary education in arithmetic and Hindi. His father, BD Birla, then initiated him into the world of business in Calcutta. The city was becoming the centre of the jute industry and the British had total control over it. In 1912, his father-in-law, M. Somani, helped him start a brokerage business. Birla was just about 15 or 16. He had come over to Calcutta from Pilani village in Rajasthan. He stayed in the one-room tenement for a long time. He had to sleep, eat, drink, bathe and pray in that room itself.

He established Birla Brothers in 1918. Soon he bought an old cloth mill in Delhi and later diversified into jute. In 1921 he established a cotton mill in Gwalior and in 1923–24 he bought the Keshoram Cotton Mills. By 1939, Birla Brothers made such progress that they were ranked among the top dozen industrialists of those times.

In many areas of business, they ended the dominance of the English and established new industries. The establishment of jute industries is one such example. In connection with the establishment of HINDALCO, he said that he had to undergo a lot of trouble to establish the company and also had to face many problems with the bureaucracy. On the other hand, he was receiving invitations from countries like England and Germany, which wanted him to be a part of their country's development plans. At that time Birla was 60 years old and he felt that he did not want to set industries overseas. He was also of the opinion that aid from the government should not be sought for the establishment of industries.

Birla was actively involved in the freedom struggle and social welfare activities. Gandhiji not only considered Ghanshyam Das Birla his friend, but also a significant adviser. In this way Birla became a link between the British and Gandhiji for talks and advice on matters of India's welfare. Birla also started 400 primary schools in a span of just one year. The driving force behind this endeavour was probably the fact that he himself never had the opportunity to receive proper education. He established the Birla Science Institute in Pilani.

A peek into his life reveals that his way of thinking was different from traditional business people. His approach was modern. But he also listened to the arguments of his critics.

Although he believed in casteism, his life is proof enough that he fully cooperated with the welfare programmes initiated by Gandhiji for the betterment of Harijans. He founded the Harijan Sevak Sangh and remained the president of the institution for many years. In those days, Indians who went abroad had to do penance. Birla opposed this orthodox custom. He, in fact, broke a number of Marwari traditions. On 30 January 1948, Gandhiji was assassinated at Birla House in New Delhi. So Birla dedicated that property to the nation.

G.D. Birla passed away on 11 June 1983, while on a visit to London.

Dhirubhai Ambani

Founder of the Reliance Group

(1932–2002)

Dhirajlal Hirachand Ambani had expanded his business empire to such dizzy heights in the 20th Century and benefited so many shareholders that other industrialists, wealthy barons and brokers felt threatened. The story of Dhirubhai Ambani is a typical rags-to-riches story. Rising from a room in a chawl to lead the establishment of a big business empire is almost like a wish fulfilled by the genie of Aladdin's lamp.

Dhirubhai Ambani was born on 28 December 1932 in Chorwad, Gujarat. In 1949 at the age of just 17, he went to Aden (now a part of Yemen) and worked for A Besse & Co, the sole distributor of Shell. In 1958 he returned to Bombay (now Mumbai) and started Reliance Commercial Corporation. Armed with only a high school degree, he established the Reliance company, a commodity trading and export house. In 1966 he started a textile mill in Naroda, Ahmedabad.

In 1977 Reliance went public. Then it had 58,000 investors. It rose to over four million equity holders. And this is all because of his intelligence and a special way of working, which had till now never been realised by other industrialists. He has also given a new direction to the Indian economic scenario. He devised a new method of collecting money from the share market on lower interest rates when other companies were taking loans from banks on high interest rates.

In 1991, the Rs 9,000-crore Hazira gas cracker plant was commissioned. Reliance diversified into infrastructure. The following year Reliance became the first Indian company to raise money in global markets with a GDR issue. In 1993 Reliance expanded into plastics and PVC. In 1994 major expansion plans for the Hazira plant were announced. Reliance became the first Indian company to touch net profits of Rs 1,000 crore. In 1996 the company diversified into power and telecom services. The following year the world's largest multi-feed cracker was commissioned in Hazira. Reliance also became the first Asian firm to raise a 100-year debt. It also began cellular services the same year. In 1999 the world's largest grassroot refinery was commissioned at Jamnagar, Gujarat.

In 1986 when he suffered a stroke, his sons Mukesh and Anil were entrusted with additional responsibility of the company.

Some Indian scholars firmly believe in the saying: *Bhagya Phalti Sarvada Na Vidya Na Cha Kausalam.* (Luck helps to prosper rather than sound education or expertise.) But it seems that the baron of Reliance Industries has proved them all wrong. His father was a Gujarati school teacher. Rising from humble beginnings, he scaled new heights and converted his small business into a force to be reckoned with in the international arena. The expansion of the Ambani empire has solely been the result of his intellect and expertise.

In 2001 he received the ET Award for Corporate Excellence for Lifetime Achievement. In 2002 Reliance Petrochemicals merged with Reliance Industries Limited.

Dhirubhai Ambani has been voted as the 'Indian Businessman of the Century' by a worldwide multimedia poll conducted between August and October 1999 by Business Barons.

Dhirubhai Ambani died on 6 July 2002 after suffering a cerebral stroke. Reliance is now an over Rs three lac crore conglomerate.

Mohan Singh Oberoi

The Grand Hotelier

(1898–2002)

Legendary hotelier Mohan Singh Oberoi officially declared that he was born in 1900 because he did not want to be known as a person of the 19th Century. And when he died in 2002, many said that he was a man of the 21st Century.

What began as a dream in Rawalpindi culminated with the Oberoi chain of hotels comprising 35 hotels in seven countries. But the young teenager dared to dream and what is more significant is that he realised his dream.

MS Oberoi was born on 15 August 1898 in Bhaun. He had to leave his village to pursue further studies. Having failed the examination, he was taking a stroll on the Mall in Shimla when he came across the imposing Hotel Cecil. He asked for a job in the hotel and he was given the job of a clerk with a salary of Rs 50 per month. That was his break into the hospitality business.

Dame Luck smiled on him and a series of promotions and a switch of job later, he was working as the manager of Hotel Clarkes. It was then that Ernest Clarke, the owner of Hotel Clarkes, decided to move over to England. So in 1934, he mortgaged his wife's jewellery and with some financial help from an elderly uncle, he acquired the Clarkes Hotel from Mr Clarke for Rs 20,000.

In 1938, he acquired the 500-room Grand Hotel on a lease of Rs 8,000 per month. The city was then reeling from an outbreak of cholera. During the Second World War, the Allied troops sought refuge in the hotel. The British were pleased with his hospitality and bestowed upon him the title Rai Bahadur. Soon he made a string of acquisitions – even Hotel Flashmans, the hotel that inspired him to dream big. His first international venture was Soaltee Oberoi in Nepal in 1969.

Oberoi Group of Hotels now has a chain of five-star hotels in Melbourne, Bali, Colombo, Mauritius, Cairo, Budapest, among others. The Oberoi Group was the first to employ women in hotels.

Oberoi was elected to the Rajya Sabha twice – in 1962 and 1972, and once to the Lok Sabha in 1968. He was honoured with the Padma Bhushan in 2001. *Newsweek* named him one of its 'Elite Winners of 1978' for his valuable contribution to the world of business.

Once when he was asked what motivated him, he said, "The idea was never merely to make money. The compulsion was to think big, always to offer the best." When Oberoi turned 100, the Oberoi Group of Hotels had a range of heritage properties across the world including Melbourne's Windsor Hotel and Oberoi Maidens in India, which is a heritage building.

He once said, "I have been able to accept the challenge and make good – there is comfort in knowing that whatever little I have achieved has also helped to raise the prestige of my country." He made the best out of the opportunities and that is the secret of his success.

Ramnath Goenka

The Fearless Newspaper Baron

(1904–1991)

Ramnath Goenka was the only newspaper baron who opposed Indira Gandhi during the Emergency period. During the Emergency, not only was Goenka's Delhi office raided, all efforts were made to put an end to his empire. But Goenka thwarted these efforts with valour. The reigns of the government were in the hands of Indira Gandhi and she wielded a lot of power, but that did not deter him from opposing Indira's government. This was the first time in the history of independent India that an individual had stood up to the government.

He was born on 3 April 1904 in Darbhanga in Bihar.

Most newspapers and media personalities adopted the middle path rather than invite the wrath of the government. But Goenka refused to bow down before the whims and fancies of the government. And he emerged a winner. When India went to the polls, Indira Gandhi was badly defeated and the Janata Party came to power.

The Janata Party lauded Goenka's steadfastness. But Goenka never tried to take undue advantage of this proximity to the ruling party.

Along with the English edition of the *Indian Express*, he also brought out newspapers in Hindi and regional languages like *Jansatta* and *Loksatta*. He also published the film journal *Screen*. S. Mulgaonkar, S. Gurumurthy and Arun Shourie were some of the prominent journalists who worked for him.

Ramnath Goenka was born in a Marwari family in Darbhanga (Bihar) and was religious-minded. He went on pilgrimage to Tirupati frequently. Goenka started *Indian Express* in 1932, but he became more well known during the Emergency.

Ramnath Goenka died on 5 October 1991 in Mumbai.

N.R. Narayana Murthy

Founder of Infosys

(Born 1946)

Narayana Murthy is the founder of one of the world's most successful software giants. What is remarkable is not that the company and its business is extensive, but the fact that the company functions with a lot of discernment. As a result, when a majority of the software companies are trying to make a mark in the international arena, Murthy's company, Infosys, is conducting most of its business abroad.

Narayana Murthy started the company in 1981 along with six close associates. For some time the company's annual turnover remained Rs 50 crores, but what is remarkable is that America chose Murthy's company as the first Indian company for its trade relations. Apart from the home front, even Nasdaq, which is considered the Mecca of high-level technical companies, has rated Infosys as a top-level software company. The secret of the success of Infosys and Narayana Murthy is that they plunged into the business of computers and information technology when the time was ripe.

Narayana Murthy studied electrical engineering from Mysore University. Then he joined IIT, Kanpur for a degree in computer science. Murthy comes from a humble background. His father was a school teacher in the Kolar district of Karnataka.

It was because of his acumen that he reached such a position where his profits soared from Rs 117 million to Rs 293.52 million. The income generated outside the country increased from Rs 500 million to Rs 869 million. The company is progressing by leaps and bounds and its net worth runs into hundreds of billions.

Sabeer Bhatia

The Young Achiever

(Born 1966)

At the age of 45, the achievement of Sabeer Bhatia is remarkable. He has not only made a name for himself, but has also acquired a lot of wealth. Sabeer Bhatia's 'Hotmail' has changed the lives of people the world over. What is astounding is the fact that when he got started with 'Hotmail', he just had three clients. Today it caters to more than 220 million people worldwide.

The momentous occasion in Sabeer Bhatia's life came when Microsoft decided to buy 'Hotmail' for $400 million. This catapulted Sabeer Bhatia to fame and fortune overnight.

Bhatia was born in Chandigarh. In 1984, he joined the California Institute of Technology in the US for higher studies. Then he went to Stanford to do his Masters in electronic engineering. He tried his hand at various jobs, but the critical point in his life came in 1996 when he started 'Hotmail' along with Jack Smith of Apple Computers. After he sold 'Hotmail', Sabeer started a new company called Arzoo.com. This was shut down in June 2001 due to the downturn in business.

Men like Sabeer Bhatia have not only made a mark for themselves, but also made India proud.

Shiv Nadar

IT Entrepreneur

(Born 1945)

Among the world's renowned people connected with the world of information technology, Shiv Nadar is considered one of the greatest entrepreneurs in the field of computers. In 1975, when the whole of India had just 250 computers, he established the company HCL. Now the company has 19 branches outside India. There are a total of 30 branches of HCL and the annual turnover of the company is over 4700 million dollars. This is proof enough that Shiv Nadar worked with a lot of prudence.

In 1997, *Time* magazine praised him for his perception and rationality.

What puts Shiv Nadar apart from other industrialists is that he had the right perception about the market and could rightly guess the pulse of the international market. In his book, *Giant Killer*, Geoffrey James puts Shiv Nadar's company HCL at par with Microsoft, Hewlitt-Packard and Compaq. This tells us that his company is no less than these giant blue chip companies.

Nadar studied electronic engineering from Coimbatore and started as a system analyst. He also worked with the Delhi Cloth Mills as chief administrator. Then he established HCL. Shiv Nadar believes in the proverb 'Strike when the iron is hot'.

Harprasad Nanda

Pioneering Industrialist

(1917–1999)

Harprasad Nanda was one of the pioneers to establish industries after the independence of India. Before the partition of the country, he had established the Escorts Group of Industries at Lahore in 1944, but after Partition, he lost all his wealth and so re-established the industries in Delhi.

Harprasad Nanda was born on 9 January 1917 in Jammu. When he wanted to revive the Escorts Group in India, he was short of finances, but with his dedication, intelligence and truthfulness, he progressed. Initially, he set up a factory in Faridabad for the manufacture of agricultural implements and tractors. Then he began the manufacture of Rajdoot motorcycles. Now his company Escorts is a well known and popular brand name.

Harprasad Nanda will also be remembered for the whole-hearted determination with which he opposed the attempt of London-based NRI businessman Swraj Paul to buy off the shares of Escorts and take over the company in 1983.

Escorts Group of Companies is being looked after by his sons Rajan and Anil. Nanda's son Rajan is married to the daughter of the famous film producer and actor, the late Raj Kapoor.

Harprasad Nanda's name has been etched in the pages of history as one of the pioneering industrialists of independent India.

Laxman Rao Kirloskar

Powering the Nation

(1869–1956)

The word 'Kirloskar' brings to mind the whirring sound produced by power generators. Laxman Rao Kirloskar is one of the few industrialists who identified the fact that apart from developing the state of agriculture, it was necessary to simultaneously develop industrial strength for the welfare of the country. He felt that for the development of villages it was imperative that we invent the right tools and implements.

So initially he developed the iron plough to replace the wooden one. The plough was the primary tool used by a farmer, and a wooden one had to be replaced every year. But an iron one could last a lifetime. However, procuring the iron was a problem. So he bought old iron cannons from the King of Kolhapur.

The Kirloskar company now manufactures a number of agricultural and engineering equipment and engines. These play an important role in industries. In this way Kirloskar had a far-reaching impact on these industries. He paid attention to the fact that the machines manufactured by him were the best in quality. As a result, not only in India, he was highly respected in the world too. And this respect he earned in 1926 itself.

In 1926, he held an exhibition of his products. Many people including foreigners had seen the products for the first time. And one of them asked whether the goods were of foreign origin.

Even after so many years the capacity and quality of Kirloskar engines and other equipments have not lessened. The Kirloskar group has recently started an automobile plant for the manufacture of cars.

Laxman Rao Kirloskar's name has been etched forever among the prominent industrialists of the 20th Century.

Karsanbhai Patel

The 'Nirma' Man

(Born 1943)

There are some consumer products that have become an integral part of our life. One such product is Nirma detergent powder. There are a number of detergent powders in the market including those marketed by multinationals. But the total sales of all the other detergent powders combined is less than half the sales of Nirma. This makes it clear that the manufacturer of Nirma, Karsanbhai Patel, has displayed immense shrewdness. His life proves that if a person works hard, it is not difficult to put an idea into practice and become a success.

In 1966, Karsanbhai was working at a factory in Ahmedabad as a chemist and drawing a salary of Rs 150 per month. He found it hard to make both ends meet. So in his spare time he made detergent powder at home and went from door to door on his cycle selling his product. Soon he thought of expanding his business. So he began to sell the powder in packets. He had started a factory in the backyard of his home. Soon he began to supply the detergent to various shops in Ahmedabad. Nirma gradually became popular not only in small towns, but also in big cities. Karsanbhai's product soon made its presence felt in the Indian market. Thus Karsanbhai was able to expand his business all over the country in a short span of time.

The secret of Karsanbhai's success is that he made quality products available for the average customer at competitive prices. Consumers realised that instead of using a bar of detergent to scrub and clean dirty clothes, it was better to keep them soaked in a good and cheaper detergent. This compelled the multinational Hindustan Lever to rethink its products, strategies and policies. Today Nirma products are household names and the company's networth is around Rs.3000 crore.

Keshub Mahindra

Progressive Industrialist

(Born 1923)

Keshub Mahindra is the chairman of Mahindra & Mahindra Group of Companies. He is one of those 15 top industrialists whose age is above 75 years and one of those 10 industrialists who command a great deal of respect in the industrial world.

Mahindra & Mahindra manufactures jeeps and other vehicles which have found a place in the consumer market because of their quality and sturdiness. The vehicles are all-terrain vehicles.

Keshub Mahindra was born in Shimla. He is one of those accomplished industrialists who has not only seen the industrial progress of five decades of his company, but was also the chairman of various companies like Union Carbide, Indian Aluminium, Remington Red and Otis Elevators.

Mahindra & Mahindra Group, which was established in 1947, made quick progress. Apart from tractors, the company also manufactures other vehicles. He believed that for being successful, it was necessary that one should be organised and work in coordination. It was because of his wisdom and expertise that he is one of the leading industrialists of India.

Azim H. Premji

The Wipro Legend

(Born 1945)

India occupies a significant position in the world of Information Technology. And the most prominent company in the field of IT is Azim H. Premji's Bangalore-based company, Wipro Corporation.

Azim Hasham Premji was born in Bombay in 1945. His father owned a cooking fat manufacturing company by the name Western India Vegetable Products Ltd (Wipro). Azim Premji graduated in engineering from Stanford University. And when he returned to India in 1966, he had to take over the family business because of his father's death. Premji was a man with a vision. Instead of venturing into industrial production, he focused on consumer preferences and needs. He used attractive packaging to woo consumers and further the Wipro brand name. He also did away with middlemen and sold his products directly to the consumer, thereby increasing his profits. Contrary to other family-run businesses, he did not appoint members of his own family, but recruited management and engineering graduates. He diversified his business into bath soaps, hydraulic fluid, electrical appliances, baby products and finance.

In 1979, the American computer giant Internationl Business Machines (IBM) was denied permission to continue its operations in the country. This was when Premji ventured into computers. Soon his company became one of the world's biggest computer manufacturing companies. Then he ventured into software development, which alone accounts for a considerable portion of his company's annual sales.

With an estimated personal wealth of $35 billion, Azim Premji is one of the world's richest men.

Sir Shri Ram

Famous Industrialist

(1883–1963)

Sir Shri Ram started his career as an assistant secretary in the Delhi Cloth & General Mills, on a salary of rupees one hundred per month. By the time he died, he was one of the noted industrialists of the country. He got the job in Delhi Cloth Mills only because his father Madan Mohan was also working there.

Delhi Cloth Mills was at that time owned by the Gurwala family. Gurwala was a money-lender to the Nawab of Avadh and the Mughals in 1857. The family was ruined during the Bank Crises of 1913. At that time, even a prominent bank like People's Bank closed down. The Delhi Cloth Mills also passed through a great crisis in 1917. However, it managed to survive when it got orders to manufacture tents for the British Army during the First World War.

It is to the credit of Sir Shri Ram that he brought this Cloth Mill into the forefront of north Indian mills. Sir Shri Ram was an able administrator. He had great knowledge of raw materials and cotton which was required for his mill. His idol was Tata. He engaged retired civil servants like Dr Dharamveer in the management of the mill. Dr Dharamveer had occupied prominent government posts when in service.

In 1930, he established a sugar mill in Daurala, UP. Today many diversified concerns of Delhi Cloth Mills are spread over various places in India, prominent among them being Bengal Potteries, Jai Engineering Works, Usha Sewing Machines, Shri Ram Fertilisers, etc. It was diligent, untiring hard work, iron will-power and great ambition that enabled a man, who himself once earned Rs100 a month, to employ thousands of people.

Ardeshir Burjorji Godrej

Founder of the Godrej Empire

(1868–1936)

Among the builders of modern Indian industry, Ardeshir Burjorji Godrej, the founder of the Godrej Group, was a true innovator, a pioneer and a visionary.

Innovation was born out of his innate desire to be a *swadeshi* manufacturer. But *swadeshi* did not merely mean boycott of British goods. It meant utilising one's resources and genius to create something that was truly Indian. Driven by patriotic passion, Godrej began to work on a commodity that was to make Godrej a household name: the lock. Ardeshir Burjorji Godrej was born in Broach on 26 March 1868. He was educated in Bombay, and was a practising lawyer. Once he went to Zanzibar to plead a case for his client. He argued well but at a particular point, in order to win the case for his client, he had to twist the facts, which he found immoral and unethical. He not only lost the case but also bade farewell to the legal profession.

During the first decade of the 20th Century, the nationalist leaders gave a call for *swadeshi* and boycott. Ardeshir pleaded with the Indian leaders that the political battle even if won, would not amount to much so long as we were in the bondage of industrial slavery. India had to become economically self-reliant, otherwise freedom would remain a distant dream. He argued that in order to achieve this, instead of depending on goods manufactured abroad, we had to utilise our own manpower, establish our own industry and use our own raw materials.

He therefore decided to start manufacturing surgical instruments in India. The problem, however, was the capital. He required a few thousand rupees and he didn't have the money. Then, he approached Merwanji Cama, a multimillionaire and asked for a loan. Mr Cama readily obliged and gave him a few thousand rupees. Ardeshir manufactured the surgical instruments and they were up to the mark. The snag, however, was that chemists would not sell surgical instruments made in India and the venture flopped.

A lesser person would have given up the fight but Ardeshir was made of different stuff. He found out that making locks and safes was an ancient art going back 4,000 years and Indian workmen were already preparing locks of different kinds. He studied the technology thoroughly and decided to manufacture locks the likes of which India had never seen before and which would vie with locks imported from foreign countries. Since then, the Godrej family has never looked back. They went from strength to strength selling different varieties of locks and later manufacturing safes and bank lockers.

Ardeshir adopted the latest technology in his factory but in his organisation there was not a single foreigner. When Jawaharlal Nehru visited the factory, he immediately noticed this and wondered how the House of Godrej would carry on without a foreign expert. Ardeshir assured him that he had full faith in the competence of his artisans and they had delivered the goods. Since then, the Godrej family has come a long way, diversified into personal-care products, food processing machine tools, office systems, etc. but the basic principles of honesty, integrity and service have always remained unchanged.

When Ardeshir Godrej went to Merwanji Cama to repay the loan, the latter waived it away. The only stipulation was that he should take his nephew Boyce into the Godrej concern and add his name to the firm. Ardeshir readily agreed. The nephew soon lost interest and dropped out but the name "Boyce" continued.

Having succeeded at making the first rudimentary security system, Godrej opened shop, setting up the Godrej & Boyce Mfg Co in 1897. At a time when the 'Made in England' tag was enough to sell goods, Godrej was able to break the customer's mental barrier.

A Century later, his spirit of innovation still drives his group.

Scientists

Jagadish Chandra Bose

Discoverer of Life in Plants

(1858–1937)

The contribution of Jagadish Chandra Bose cannot be bound by time or Century. He has several firsts to his credit, but he was so engrossed in his work that he never pursued fame.

Dr Jagadish Chandra Bose was a scientist of rare intellect. The extent of work carried out by Bose was significant because no other scientist had done any work in this field. And he will be remembered for another important deed. He always made an attempt to get Indian officials the same respect and salary as their British counterparts. He struggled for three years and was finally successful in getting the same salary as an English professor.

Jagadish Chandra Bose was born in Memansingh district (now in Bangladesh) of West Bengal on 30 November 1858. His father was a collector. At the age of 13, he went to Calcutta (now Kolkata) for higher education and, in 1880, he received admission at Christ College in Cambridge. At Cambridge, he worked with a professor of physics, Roley. It was here that he befriended the famous biologist Dr Vines and became interested in biology.

In 1885, he returned to Calcutta and was appointed professor of physical science at Presidency College.

After dedicating himself to teaching, his interest in conducting research was sparked. In 1915, he left the university to found the Bose Research Institute, Calcutta. He first conducted research on electricity and with the help of wires created waves that made a telephone, which was kept at a distance of 75 feet, ring. His experiment on the quasi-optical properties of very short radio waves led him to make improvements on the cohere, an early form of radio detector, which contributed to the development of solid-state physics. However, in spite of the fact that Bose studied electric waves first, it was Marconi who got the credit.

Dr Bose then switched over to botany and began to study plants very minutely. For his research, he invented a device called the cryocograph. This device measured the development of a plant. He constructed automatic recorders that could register even the slightest movements. He also developed other devices to measure the effect of sleep, air, food and poison. With the help of his research, he concluded that plants also slept, felt joy and pain like other living beings.

Because of his exemplary works, Dr Bose was made a member of the Royal Society of London. He went to England and America a number of times and demonstrated his research with the help of his devices. In 1915, he pooled in all his resources and established the Bose Research Institute. He was able to interest the world's scientists in his work and his fame grew. Rabindranath Tagore remained one of his steadfast friends.

His published works include *Response in the Living and Non-living* and *The Nervous Mechanism of Plants.*

M.S. Swaminathan

Father of the Green Revolution

(Born 1925)

India is a land of villages and a majority of the people are involved in agriculture. However, the land is prone to droughts and famines. During the reign of the British, the people led a very miserable life. Famines were frequent and there was no respite from them. The main reason for the sad plight of the people was that they were using age-old methods of farming. Nobody paid attention to the development of better seeds.

It was Monkombu Sambisivan Swaminathan who first realised that developing better varieties of seeds was the only solution to make India self-reliant in crops. He accepted a variety of the Mexican wheat to solve the Indian crop crisis. This helped increase India's crop production. Therefore, Swaminathan is often referred to as the harbinger of India's Green Revolution. Since then India has become so self-reliant that there has been a steady increase in crop production and the country also exports crops.

Dr Swaminathan was born on 7 August 1925 at Kumbhkonam town in Tamil Nadu in the family of a nationalist doctor, Samishivan Swaminathan. Dr Swaminathan dedicated himself completely to agriculture and agriculture-based projects. For five years he worked with an international rice institute and returned to India in 1988. Then he was appointed the director of Pusa Institute, the director of Indian Agricultural Research Centre, and the Secretary of the Agricultural Ministry.

Along with the Royal Society of London, 14 other prominent international science centres granted him fellowship. Many universities also honoured him with doctorates. In 1967, he was honoured with the Padma Shri and in 1972 with the Padma Bhushan. The country gave accolades to a person who never tried to steal the limelight. In 1971, he also received the Magsaysay Award for Community Leadership. He received the Albert Einstein Award in 1986, the first World Food Prize in 1987, the Tyler Prize of the United States in 1991, Japan's Honda Prize for Eco-technology in 1994, France's *Ordre du Merite Agricole* (Order of Merit in Agriculture) in 1997, the Henry Shaw Medal of the Missouri Botanical Garden (USA) in 1998, the Volvo International Environment Award and the UNESCO Gandhi Gold Award in 1999. In 1999, *Time* magazine voted him one of the 20 most influential Asians of the 20th Century.

Apart from being a well-known agricultural scientist, Dr Swaminathan was also an efficient administrator. He played a significant role in the handling of various plans and projects. Because of his undaunted efforts, India's food problems were resolved and his fame spread. Nobel laureate and famous agricultural scientist Dr Norman E Borlaug has also praised Dr Swaminathan's efforts.

In the early 1990s he established the MS Swaminathan Research Foundation in Madras (now Chennai) with the funds he received from various awards and prizes. The research centre has done pioneering work towards job-led economic growth strategy in Indian villages. It is based on a pro-nature and pro-women orientation to technology development and dissemination of information. The contribution of Swaminathan and the Centre has received international recognition. Swaminathan holds the UNESCO Chair in Eco-technology with Responsibility for South Asia.

If we consider the efforts of Dr Swaminathan in entirety, we will realise that he has made an immense contribution for the development of the rural sector. He was able to inspire the common Indian farmer to accept new farming methods. The country has witnessed a dramatic progress in plant conservation and development, which has resulted in a great revolution in crop production.

Sir C.V. Raman

Prominent Indian Scientist

(1888–1970)

Chandrasekhara Venkata Raman is considered one of those prominent personalities of the 20th Century who was not disturbed by the trials and tribulations in life and remained steadfast, thus becoming successful in achieving his aim. He was the first Indian scientist to win the Nobel Prize for Physics in 1930 for the discovery that when light traverses a transparent medium, some of the light that is deflected changes its wavelength. This phenomenon is now called the Raman Effect.

C.V. Raman was born on 7 November 1880 at Thiruvanaikkaval near Tiruchirappalli, Tamil Nadu into an orthodox South Indian family. He was a brilliant student. At the age of 11 he completed his matriculation. After graduating from Presidency College, Madras (now Chennai) at the age of 15, he wanted to go to England. But he was disqualified on medical grounds. So after acquiring a master's degree in Physics from the college in 1907, Raman joined as an assistant accountant general in the finance department of the Indian Government.

He was posted to Calcutta. It was here that he discovered the Indian Association for the Cultivation of Science, where he began doing his research work, outside office hours. In 1917, Sir Ashutosh Mukherjee appointed him the Palit Professor of Physics at the newly-endowed chair in the Calcutta University.

The turning point of his life came when he had the opportunity to go to Europe in 1921 as a representative of Calcutta University at a science meet. He wondered why the water of the Mediterranean Sea had such a dark shade of blue. Light became the subject of Raman's study. Studying the scattering of light in various substances, in 1928 he discovered that when a beam of light of one frequency illuminates a transparent object

– solid, liquid or gaseous – a small portion of the light emerges at right angles to the original direction, and some of this light is of different frequencies than that of the incident light. These so-called Raman-frequencies are equal to the infrared frequencies for the scattering material and caused by the exchange of energy between the light and the material. His discovery was named the "Raman Effect". He used a mercury arc and a spectrograph for his study.

In 1929, Raman received knighthood. In 1930 he became the first Indian to win the Nobel Prize for Physics. He described his experience thus, "When the Nobel award was announced, I saw it as a personal triumph, an achievement, a recognition for a very remarkable discovery, for reaching the goal I had pursued for seven years. But when I sat in that crowded hall and I saw the sea of western faces surrounding me, and I, the only Indian, in my turban and closed coat, it dawned on me that I was really representing my country and my people. I felt truly humble when I received the prize from King Gustav; it was a moment of great emotion, but I could restrain myself. Then I turned round and saw the British Union Jack under which I had been sitting and it was then that I realised that my poor country, India, did not have even a flag of her own – and it was this that triggered off my complete breakdown."

In 1933, he joined the Indian Institute of Science, Bangalore and served as its director until 1937. Next, he was the head of the department of physics until 1947. Then he retired from the Indian Institute and founded the Raman Research Institute in Bangalore. The land was a gift from the then king of Mysore. He founded the *Indian Journal of Physics* and the Indian Academy of Sciences. He was closely associated with many Indian research institutions of his time.

Raman also did some outstanding research on musical instruments like the violin and the veena. His research on the veena was documented in the work, *On the Mechanical Theory of Vibrations of Musical Instruments of the Violin Family.*

He was honoured with the Bharat Ratna in 1954. In 1957 he won the International Lenin Prize. He died on 21 November 1970 in Bangalore.

Dr Homi Jehangir Bhabha

Father of India's Nuclear Programme

(1909-1966)

Dr Homi Bhabha was not only India's eminent physicist, he was also the principal architect of India's nuclear programme. Dr Bhabha realised the importance of developing alternate energy sources for India because natural sources were limited. But Pt Nehru felt that in a poor country like India, the priorities of the government were very different from developing nuclear power. It took a lot of convincing by JRD Tata and Homi Bhabha for Pt Nehru to agree to it.

Dr Homi Jehangir Bhabha was born in a rich, aristocratic Parsi family on 30 October 1909 in Bombay. After his formal education in India, he joined the University of Cambridge to study mechanical engineering. After obtaining his degree in 1930, he joined Cavendish Laboratories in Cambridge to carry out research. In 1935, he obtained his doctorate.

He had come to India on a holiday, when the Second World War broke out in Europe. As all of Europe was in turmoil, he decided to stay back in India. It was during his stay in India that he met Nobel laureate Sir C.V. Raman, who was then the director of the Indian Institute of Science, Bangalore. He asked Dr Bhabha to join the institute. So in 1940, Dr Bhabha joined the Indian Institute of Science as a reader in Physics.

Being from an aristocratic family, Dr Bhabha had a western upbringing. But he envisaged a bright future for India. He realised the importance of developing nuclear energy for the industrial growth of India. So in 1945, Bhabha founded the Tata Institute of Fundamental Research (TIFR). The funds were arranged by JRD Tata. In 1948, the Atomic Energy Commission was instituted by the Government of India and Dr Bhabha was appointed its Chairman. He later founded the Atomic Energy Establishment in Trombay.

His contribution towards India's nuclear programme earned him world renown. In 1955, he was appointed the president of the United Nations Conference for Peaceful Uses of Atomic Energy. Between 1960 and 1963, he served as the president of the International Union of Pure and Applied Physics.

However, the eminent physicist died in an air crash over Mont Blanc in the Swiss Alps on 24 January 1966. The Atomic Energy Establishment in Trombay was renamed the Bhabha Atomic Research Centre (BARC) in memory of its founder.

Dr Vikram Sarabhai

Scientist, Industrialist, Educationist

(1919–1971)

Dr Vikram Sarabhai is called the father of Indian space research. He not only developed Indian rocketry, he developed scientific research centres to carry out research in the field and remained attached to these organisations till the end. From the development of uranium for nuclear energy to the development of rockets and missiles to the installation of nuclear power stations, he was involved in all the projects. Dr Vikram Sarabhai strongly advocated that India should not sign the Non- Proliferation Treaty till the country did not develop nuclear weapons.

Vikram Sarabhai believed that development of science was of utmost importance for the progress of the country. He was aware of all the hurdles that would hinder the growth of the country. For example, he wanted scientists and engineers to come forward and join hands to find a solution for the shortage of water and the problem of droughts in the country.

The contribution made by Dr Sarabhai towards space and nuclear research in the 20th Century is stupendous. He established the Indian Space Research Organisation (ISRO) at Thumba, a remote fishing village near Trivandrum in Kerala and became its first chairman. The centre has developed a number of satellites that have helped India take giant strides in the field of mass communications and weather forecasting.

Vikram Ambalal Sarabhai was born on 12 August 1919, in Ahmedabad into a well-to-do industrialist family. When he was only two years old, Rabindranath Tagore predicted that the child would one day earn a lot of fame and recognition.

Mathematics and science were his favourite subjects. He was also deeply inclined towards physics. In 1936, he completed his Intermediate from Gujarat College, Ahmedabad. In 1936, he joined Cambridge University and in 1939, at the age of 20, he passed the Tripos examination in physics. When the Second World War broke out, he returned to India. Here he had the opportunity of meeting Sir C.V. Raman and undertook research in cosmic rays under his guidance. Once the War was over, he returned to Cambridge to pursue his doctorate and wrote the thesis on *Cosmic Ray Investigations in Tropical Latitudes*. When he came back to India, he founded the Physical Research Laboratory in Ahmedabad.

He also established the Ahmedabad Textile Industries' Research Association (ATIRA) in 1947, which tried to solve technical problems faced by the textile industry. He looked after the centre till 1956. He established Sarabhai Chemicals, the first pharmaceutical company in the country to make basic drugs. It was because of his efforts that the Indian Institute of Management was instituted in 1962. The same year he established the Indian National Committee for Space Research, which was later renamed the Indian Space Research Organisation (ISRO). He also set up the Thumba Equatorial Rocket Launching Station.

Besides being involved in the research of solar radiation in the Physical Research Laboratory at Ahmedabad, he also worked on the development of nuclear energy, software technology, space research, physical sciences and astronomy. He took over as the chairman of the Atomic Energy Commission in 1966, after the death of Dr Homi Bhabha. The development of India's first artificial satellite was done at the Physical Research Laboratory. He encouraged the development of indigenous nuclear technology for defence purposes.

In 1966 he was honoured with the Padma Shri. He died prematurely in his sleep, while visiting Thumba on 30 December 1971. In 1972 he was posthumously awarded the Padma Vibhushan.

Dr M. Visvesvaraya

Engineer, Administrator and Educationist

(1861–1962)

Dr Mokshagundam Visvesvaraya always strove for a better tomorrow. In this, he found a friend in Krishnaraj Vadiyar, the King of Mysore. Krishnaraj Vadiyar tried to improve the lot of his subjects with the help of Dr Visvesvaraya. Today, Mysore is a part of Karnataka. In the beginning of the 20th Century, when the rulers of other princely states were indifferent to the plight of their subjects, the King of Mysore took steps to educate his subjects and put the state on the path to industrial progress. He chalked out a number of welfare programmes and entrusted the task of turning his ideas into reality to Dr Visvesvaraya. The duo transformed Mysore into a centre of industrial, agricultural and other strongholds.

Dr Visvesvaraya worked on several irrigation projects in the city. As an engineer, Dr Visvesvaraya also handled many water drainage and irrigation projects in other parts of the country. It is because of his successful projects that Dr Visvesvaraya achieved a place of honour among prominent personalities and was honoured with the Bharat Ratna. His work provided the necessary infrastructure for the industrial growth of India.

Dr Visvesvaraya was born on 15 September 1860 at a village in Chikvalpur district of Mysore. His father Shrinivas Shastri did not have the resources to educate his children, but Dr Visvesvaraya showed signs of ingenuity right from childhood. He gave tuitions to young children to provide for his own education. He obtained a scholarship in college and completed his BSC from Bangalore University with flying colours. Then he joined the Science College at Poona. One advantage of joining the college was that the candidate who stood first in the college was directly appointed as Assistant Engineer in the Public Works Department (PWD).

So Visvesvaraya joined the PWD when he was 23. His fruitful life began from here.

He had the distinction of turning many impossible ideas into reality, because of which he was praised even by British officers. After Bombay, he had the opportunity of working in Nasik. Then he was sent to Khandesh. A perennial river at Dhuliya in Khandesh caused much woe to the people. He not only harnessed the river waters to prevent floods, but also made arrangements to provide safe drinking water for the people of Khandesh. Next, he was entrusted with the task of providing water to Poona and later to the northern part of Sakkhar in Sindh. The project was difficult to accomplish, but under his supervision, manufacturing of tanks and drains was completed on time. The project was to carry waters of the Indus River to a tank built over a mountain and then to the town. When the Governor of Bombay (Sindh was then a part of Bombay) inaugurated the project, he showered Visvesvaraya with praise. Such successful projects made him a well-known figure.

So he was promoted to the post of superintending engineer. He then worked on projects in Bangalore, Poona, Mysore, Karachi, Baroda, Gwalior, Indore, Kolhapur, Sangli, Surat, Nasik, Nagpur, Dharwad, Bijapur and other cities and solved the problem of water shortage in these areas.

The King of Mysore, Vadiyar IV, was highly impressed by his works and called him over to Mysore. At first, he appointed Visvesvaraya the chief engineer of his state and later, the *diwan*. He built the Krishnarajsagar dam on the river Cauvery, which provided water for irrigation and for hydro-electricity. This was the first hydro-electrical project in India.

In September 1961, when he had completed 101 years, he was asked the secret of his long life and he exclaimed that the secret was his work being done on time. He also wrote many books that shed light on his projects. One of his books, *Reconstructing India*, is a trendsetting book for architects and builders.

Dr Visvesvaraya died on 14 April 1962 in Bangalore at the age of 101.

Dr Raja Ramanna

Father of the Indian Atomic Bomb

(1925–2004)

Dr Raja Ramanna is one of the prominent scientists who helped India in making the atom bomb. In the modern age, the potential of the atom bomb cannot be underestimated. Till a few decades, the country had to look up to other nations for all essential supplies. It was in 1944 that Dr Homi Jehangir Bhabha said, "In a few years from now, when we will become successful in producing nuclear energy on a vast scale, we will not be required to look up to others. In fact, we'll prepare our own experts." It was as a result of Dr Bhabha's foresight that we had an expert in nuclear physics like Dr Raja Ramanna. The Tarapur nuclear energy centre was developed because of his efforts.

Ramanna's formal education was completed in Mysore. Then he went to Bangalore and Madras for further studies. After completing his Intermediate from St Joseph's College in Bangalore, Ramanna joined Christian College in Madras for his BSc (Hons.) in Physics. After MSc, he went to King's College, London for his PhD in Molecular (Nuclear) Physics. After completing his PhD in 1948, he started his research for DSc. In 1949, he joined the Tata Institute of Fundamental Research in Bombay as a professor. In 1953, he joined Bhabha Atomic Energy Centre in Trombay. It was because of Dr Bhabha's resolute attempts that the proposal of the Tarapur nuclear reactor was approved. The construction of the Tarapur project was looked after by Raja Ramanna at the behest of Dr Bhabha. Dr Ramanna carried out his responsibility very well. After the death of Dr Bhabha, Dr Ramanna became his worthy successor.

In 1983, he was appointed the chairman of the Atomic Energy Commission and the secretary of the Atomic Energy Department by the Government of India. On 31 January 1987, he relinquished both posts. Then with financial assistance from France, Dr Ramanna and Tata constituted the National Institute of Science, Bangalore.

Dr Ramanna was born on 28 January 1925 in Mysore, Karnataka. His father, B. Ramanna, worked at the court of Mysore. His mother, Rukmini Amma, was the daughter of the district judge. First he was called Krishnaraj, later he was called Raja. Raja Ramanna has three brothers and two sisters and is the youngest of six siblings. He died on 24 September 2004 and left a trail of technological innovations to be pursued for a global presence.

Dr A.P.J. Abdul Kalam

Father of India's Missile Programme/
President of India

(Born 1931)

Friends and associates of Avul Pakir Jainulabdeen Abdul Kalam say that he may not be 100 per cent, but he is at least 200 per cent Indian. He has helped India build its missile muscle. He developed and successfully launched *Agni* and *Prithvi*, the two indigenously developed ballistic missiles that brought both China and Pakistan within India's missile range. But this scientist did not develop the missiles for the country's offensive purposes, but to strengthen its defence. The world now recognises India as a potent force.

Abdul Kalam was born into a Tamil Muslim family in a town named Dhanushkodi in district Rameswaram of Tamil Nadu in 1931. His father rented boats to fishermen. His quest for knowledge was inspired by one of his relatives who had a newspaper agency. Newspapers from around the country came to Rameswaram and Abdul Kalam used to gather news and information from them. This instilled in him the desire to seek knowledge. Abdul Kalam's father was a religious person and his mother was a woman with respect for traditional values. His parents and the serene atmosphere of Rameswaram left a deep impact on young Abdul Kalam's mind.

Initially Abdul Kalam studied in Rameswaram. After completing his twelfth class examinations from St Joseph's College in Tiruchirapalli, he wished to study engineering. So he joined the Madras Institute of Technology. At one time he nursed the desire of becoming a pilot. He started his career with the Defence Research and Development Organisation (DRDO) in 1958. He later moved on to the Indian Space Research Organisation (ISRO) in 1963. He helped India launch the 35-kg *Rohini I* satellite on a low-earth orbit with the help of Satellite Launch Vehicle III in July 1981. After being associated with ISRO for 19 years, he again moved to DRDO in 1982. It was Dr Raja Ramanna who asked him to take charge of India's Integrated Guided Missile Development Programme. Here he developed the short-range and intermediate-range ballistic missiles *Prithvi* and *Agni*.

Kalam led India's successful underground nuclear weapons' tests, which were held in May 1998.

He has also written four books: *Wings of Fire, India 2020 – A Vision for the New Millennium, My Journey* and *Ignited Minds – Unleashing the Power Within India*.

Abdul Kalam is a multifaceted personality. Apart from being a scientist, he is also a musician. He plays the Rudra Veena. He was honoured with the Padma Bhushan in 1981. He was honoured with the Bharat Ratna, the country's highest civilian award, in 1997. He was President of India from July 2002 to July 2007.

Dr Kalam is currently a visiting professor at Indian Institute of Management Ahmedabad, Chancellor of Indian Institute of Space Science and Technology, Thiruvananthapuram, professor of Aerospace Engineering at Anna University, Chennai, visiting professor of Indian Institute of Management, Indore and senior faculty member at many other academic and research institutions in India.

Social Reformers

Maharishi Karve

Social Reformer

(1858–1962)

Maharishi Dhondu Keshav Karve not only gave a new lease of life to innumerable widows, but also started a revolution for women's education and upliftment in the whole of Maharashtra.

Maharishi Karve was born on 18 April 1858 in a small village, Sheravali, of Konkan district. He had special interest in education, but getting an education was difficult in those days.

At the age of 15, he was married to 9-year-old Radhabai. At the age of 23, he passed his matric from Mumbai. Four years later, he graduated from Elphinston College. Unlike other young people of his age, he did not want to serve the British Government, so he decided to take up teaching as a profession. Around this time, he was devastated by the news of his wife's death in the village. At the same time, Gopal Krishna Gokhale invited him to join Ferguson College in Poona, as professor of mathematics. He soon became the most admired teacher of his college.

Leading a single life soon made him feel the need for a companion. When the talk of a second marriage came up, he expressed the desire to marry a widow. The British Government had then officially declared remarriage of widows as legal. However, society did not permit the remarriage of widows. Ramabai, a prominent reformist, had started a centre called *Sharda Sadan* to educate widows. It was here that the younger sister of one of Karve's friends, Narhari Pant, was seeking education. The young widow was Godavari. She was married at the age of eight and three months later she had become a child widow. On 13 March 1893 Karve married Godavari at the residence of Dr Ambedkar Bhandarkar, a famous scholar. The bride was given a new name – Anandibai.

114

The marriage was solemnised, but society did not accept it and boycotted him. He rallied the thinkers of Poona to garner support and went from village to village to campaign for the cause of widows. In 1896, at a village named Hingne, he started a home for young orphan girls in a hut. Land was allocated for the home and funds poured in. Now a permanent home stands in place of the hut.

When Maharishi Karve came across a Japanese journal, he realised that there were universities meant for women. So he decided to start a similar university in India. He left Ferguson College and totally dedicated himself to the setting up of such a university. Sir Vithaldas Thackersay, a famous industrialist, donated Rs 15 lakhs for the university in memory of his mother.

This donation helped speed up the project. In 1920, the university, Maharishi Karve Stree Shikshan Sanstha, was formally inaugurated. Karve also went to foreign countries to garner funds for the university. His wife Anandibai stood steadfast by his side.

After Independence, the university was recognised by the government. In 1958, he was awarded the Bharat Ratna. He died on 9 November 1962, at the grand old age of 105 years.

Baba Amte

Social Activist

(1914–2008)

It is difficult to put Baba Amte into the category of a saint or a social activist or even as a combination of the two. Baba Amte was only one of his kind, so it is all the more difficult to compare him with anyone else in the world. Baba Amte's spirit of sacrifice and service was so high that he often forgot his own worries and strives for the betterment of the underprivileged and the needy.

Despite suffering from cervical spondylitis that made it difficult for him to sit and stand straight, he worked for the welfare of leprosy patients, who are usually looked down upon by society. Most people are unaware that the disease is now curable, so whenever they see a leper, a feeling of aversion or sympathy is evoked in them. Most parts of the body of the victims like fingers, toes, ears and nose are reduced to stubs, after a period of time, because of the disease. Yet Baba Amte cared for them.

Apart from this, he was involved in other social activities too. He carried just a mat and a walking stick with him. Besides these personal belongings, he wore just two pieces of clothing – a pair of shorts spun out of Khadi and a sleeveless vest.

Former President K.R. Narayanan had honoured him with the 'Gandhi Peace Prize' that included prize money of Rs 1 crore. He spent the entire sum on the social uplift of the downtrodden.

Baba Amte was born Murlidhar Devidas Amte in Hinganghat, Wardha district, Maharashtra on 24 December 1914 into a family of *jagirdars* (landowners). Even as a child, Baba Amte was compassionate towards his servants and the lower classes. He studied law and set up practice in Wardha, which soon flourished. In 1942, when the nation responded to the call of Gandhiji and many prominent leaders were imprisoned, he organised lawyers to plead cases of imprisoned leaders. He was arrested. It was around this time that he saw a leper in Warora and that changed the course of his life. He gave up his profession and began to work for the uplift of lepers and the downtrodden.

In 1949, Baba Amte founded Anandvan for the rehabilitation of lepers who were shunned by society. The sprawling 50 acres of barren land soon became a self-sufficient centre with its own university, hospital, technical units, orphanage, dairy and farmlands.

In the 1980s, Baba Amte launched two *Bharat Jodo* movements to promote national integration. In 1985, he went on a tour from Kashmir to Kanyakumari. In 1988, he undertook a tour from Assam to Gujarat. In 1989, he established the ashram called Nijibal ("inner strength"), as a mark of protest against the construction of the Sardar Sarovar Dam in the Narmada Valley and the resultant displacement of tribals from the area.

For his humanitarian work, he was honoured with the Padma Shri in 1971, the Rashtriya Bhushan in 1978, the Padma Vibhushan in 1986 and the Magsaysay Award in 1988.

Due to his health problems during the last 15 years of his life, most of the work was handled by his son, Prakash Amte.

In 2007, he was diagnosed with leukemia. Baba Amte died in Anandvan on 9 February 2008. Respecting his wishes, his body was buried instead of being cremated, the traditional funeral of Hindus.

Baba Amte is remembered for his contribution towards rehabilitation and empowerment of poor people suffering from leprosy.

Vinoba Bhave

Founder of the Bhoodan Movement

(1895–1982)

Acharya Vinoba Bhave not only remained away from politics, he also remained away from publicity. Not only that, he remained detached from all the major events that rocked India and had even given up reading newspapers. So what were the character traits that make him an eminent personality? The significance of his work can be estimated from the fact that although India is an agriculture-based country, the majority of farmers do not even have a patch of land to call their own. Vinoba Bhave's attention was drawn towards this problem and he went on a campaign to ask big farmers to contribute land for landless farmers – a revolution that was named *Bhoodan* – gift of land. He collected land from landlords and gave it away to landless farmers.

It all began one day when he was touring the villages of Andhra Pradesh to appeal for land for Harijans (low-caste Hindus) and a landholder offered him a part of his land. It was then that the idea of the land-gift movement was conceived. Vinobaji held prayer meetings like Gandhiji. So that evening, after the prayer meeting, Vinobaji put forward a request for 80 acres of land from the people of the village. Such was the influence of Vinobaji's words that one of the wealthiest farmers of the village donated not 80, but 100 acres of land. And this was how the Bhoodan Movement began.

Working on Gandhiji's principle of *ahimsa*, or non-violence, he went from village to village appealing for the gift of land from wealthy landowners. He believed that land reform could be secured not by government action, but by the change of heart of the people. Then he went on a *padyatra* (walking tour), across the nation for collecting more land. He went to Bihar and sought the help of Jayprakash Narayan (JP). Bihar had a lot of wealthy landlords. With the help of JP, Vinobaji was able to collect hundreds of acres of land. He toured the country for some 14 years. He visited 45,000 villages and met millions of people and collected about 1,70,000 hectares of land, which he donated to poor farmers.

There have been examples in history where great men had to face troubles on their path towards progress. Vinobaji also had his share of trials and tribulations. His ambition was not just to provide poor Harijans with land but to elevate their financial and social status. So wherever he went, he tried to help Harijans get back into mainstream India and be accepted in society. Thus, he wanted them to be allowed into temples and in many places he faced resentment due to this.

During his *padyatra*, he also established many ashrams. His work was similar to that of Shankaracharya. As heir to Gandhiji's legacy, Vinobaji not only kept alive spiritualism but took it further and gave it a new direction.

His critics claimed that through the Bhoodan Movement, Vinobaji was encouraging the fragmentation of land and thus hindering the growth of large-scale agriculture. Later, he encouraged *gramdan*, where villagers pooled their land and worked as a co-operative.

Vinayak Narahari Vinoba was born on 11 September 1895 in Gagode, Gujarat into a high-caste Chitpavan Brahmin family. His father Narahari and mother Rukmani Devi were extremely religious people. While doing household chores, his mother chanted bhajans sung by Marathi saints. She called him Vinay. Little did she realise that her son would grow up to be a true replica of *vinay* – humility. Even as a young child, Vinobaji was unlike his peers. After his early education he passed his matric in 1913 from Baroda and took admission in Intermediate. He was able to learn by heart anything that he read for the first time. He read books on religion, literature and history from the famous library of Baroda. He was also interested in mathematics. In 1916 he gave up his studies to join Gandhiji's ashram.

One day, while sitting with his mother in the kitchen, he burnt all his certificates. When his mother asked him the reason, he replied that he did not require them, as his direction in life was different. Then he went to Kashi and studied Sanskrit. It was around this time that Madan Mohan Malaviya had established the Kashi Hindu University. Malaviya invited Gandhiji to the institution. Gandhiji had just returned from South Africa. Gandhiji inaugurated the University and gave an inaugural speech. When Vinoba read the text of the speech in the newspapers the next day, he began to yearn to see Gandhiji in person.

He went to meet Gandhiji at an ashram in Kochrab. As per Gandhiji's wishes, Vinobaji took charge of the old age home at Sabarmati. The meditation, penance and study he did during the period, put him in the category of learned men. Apart from looking after the home, he was actively involved in the other constructive works of Gandhiji, like the manufacture of Khadi, basic education, cleanliness, etc. He stayed there till 1932 and then moved over to a colony of Harijans at Nalwadi, a village that was a few kilometres away from Wardha.

Between the 1920s and 1940s he went to prison several times. In fact, he was imprisoned for five years in the 1940s for leading non-violent resistance against British rule.

He had resolved to survive on the money received from spinning his own yarn. But it was difficult to sustain oneself on this money. Lack of proper diet made him sick. Gandhiji advised him to go to a hill station, but Vinobaji went to stay at the hill of a village near river Pavnar. This helped him recover and he made Pavnar Ashram the centre of his activities.

Vinobaji participated in the satyagraha movements of Gandhiji. In the Nagpur Flag Satyagraha of 1923, he was imprisoned for 12 months. After returning from the Round Table Conference, Gandhiji was arrested in Bombay. Later Vinobaji was also put in prison. During his sentence, at the behest of fellow freedom fighters, he began to give discourses from the *Bhagavad Gita.* These discourses have been published in Hindi, English and about 20 other languages.

The fame of Vinobaji spread across the nation in 1940 during the Second World War, when India was dragged into the War without the consent of Indian leaders. During the satyagraha in 1940, Gandhiji chose Vinobaji as his worthy successor. In October, he was sent to prison. In 1942, during the Quit India Movement, he was again arrested. After the sentence, he returned to Pavnar Ashram and took over the work of village welfare. After Partition, he toured the nation to alleviate the pain of riot victims and to rehabilitate Harijans. The *Bhoodan Yojna*, published in 1953, is a series of articles that explain his philosophy of life and the movement that he started.

After Independence and the death of Gandhiji, the nation began to see him as a saint and social activist. A number of leaders and ministers consulted Vinobaji regarding spiritual and social aspects of life and political dilemmas. In 1975, he maintained a vow of silence over the issue of the involvement of his followers in the political agitation. He was thus able to persuade the government to enforce a law prohibiting the killing of cows throughout India. Cows are considered sacred by Hindus.

In spite of all these achievements, Vinobaji felt that he no longer had any special role to play, so he gave up food. On 14 November 1982, his condition deteriorated. He had also given up drinking water. The next day he died.

In 1983, he was awarded the Bharat Ratna posthumously.

Ela Bhatt

Champion of Women's Empowerment

(Born 1933)

As the economic position of women in Indian society is entirely dependent on their menfolk, their predicament is pitiable. In many states, it has been observed that in spite of working more than men, women have to depend on the men for survival.

Today efforts are being undertaken to improve the socio-economic position of women and to give them equal rights as men. The contribution made by Ela Bhatt towards the elevation of women at the grassroots level is commendable. She founded SEWA (Self-Employed Women's Association), a trade union of poor, self-employed women working in the unorganised sector. The institution has branches in all major cities of India. It provides training to women to make them self-reliant enough to look after their families. SEWA also provides assistance to backward and down-trodden sections of society. They are provided education so that they can make their lives worthwhile.

Impressed by the work of the SEWA, UNICEF and other wings of the United Nations Organisation have provided financial assistance to the organisation. Other international organisations also provide assistance to SEWA.

SEWA helps down-trodden women in finding access to the basic necessities so that they are not dependent on men. SEWA provides assistance to working women of the labour class to liberate them from the clutches of trade unions, which are dominated by men.

Ela Bhatt studied law and joined the Textile Labour Association started by Gandhiji. She strived to bring together all women working in the unorganised sector. Towards this effort, she established SEWA in 1972. Today SEWA has around 200,000 members. In 1974, she started SEWA Cooperative Bank with the aim of providing small loans to poor, down-trodden women to help them start their own earning activity. In the late 1990s, the bank had 60,000 members. Apart from its regular services, the bank also offers legal advice.

In 1986, Ela Bhatt was nominated to the Rajya Sabha. When she took over as the chairperson of the National Commission on Self-Employed Women, she drew the attention of the government towards the plight of poor women working in unorganised sectors.

For her indepth knowledge on various issues that plague society and poor women in particular, Ela Bhatt's advice is sought worldwide in matters related to banking, gender studies, policy-making and anti-poverty programmes. She was a member of the Consultative Group to Assist the Poorest of the World Bank. Between 1984 and 1988 she was the chairperson of the New York-based Women's World Banking.

Ela Bhatt has been bestowed several national and international honorary degrees and won many national and international awards. In recognition of her contribution to society, she received the Ramon Magsaysay Award for Community Leadership in 1977. In 1984, she received the Right Livelihood Award (the Alternative Nobel Prize) for "Changing the Human Environment". She was awarded the Padma Shri in 1985 and the Padma Bhushan in 1986.

Mother Teresa

Messiah of the Poor

(1910–1997)

Although Mother Teresa was born in a foreign country, her area of work was in India. She dedicated her life in the service of the 'poorest of the poor'. Mother Teresa was a Yugoslavian, but she chose India as the base of her humanitarian work, which soon spread to other countries.

Mother Teresa was born Agnes Gonxha Bojaxhiu in Skopje, Yugoslavia on 27 August 1910. By the age of 12, it was clear that she intended to become a nun. In 1928, at the age of 18, she joined the Order of Loreto nuns at a town in Ireland. Six weeks later, in 1929, she sailed to India to join a Loreto school in Calcutta (now Kolkata) as a teacher.

On 10 September 1946, when she was making a railway journey to Darjeeling, she heard the 'Voice of God' from within. She received the message that she had to dedicate her life towards the service of the poor of Calcutta. She said, "The message was clear, but I had to wait for permission from the Pope to be released from the Loreto Order and to start on my own."

After obtaining the Pope's permission, she left the Order. She gave up the black and white dress of the Order and wore a coarse blue-bordered saree. In 1948 Sister Teresa became Mother Teresa. She also became an Indian citizen. She studied nursing before moving to the slums. The plight of the poor in Calcutta could make anyone shudder. They lived in abject poverty and led miserable lives because of lack of food, clean water and medical care. The women, the aged and young children needed attention the most. Along with the poor, there were lepers who were looked down upon by society.

She founded the Missionaries of Charity in 1948 in a pilgrim hostel near the sacred Kali temple. The premises were given to her by the municipal authorities. The organisation received pontifical sanction from Pope Pius XII and formally began work in 1950. In 1965 the Order became a pontifical congregation.

Initially, money and aid were scarce. But that didn't deter her. Seeing her work, aid soon followed. She herself went out on the roads of Calcutta and picked up hapless people. The first woman she picked up was half eaten by rats and ants. But she could not be saved. She died in Mother's arms and that strengthened her resolve to dedicate her life to the cause of the poor.

Then she started Nirmal Hriday (Place of the Pure Heart) in the empty halls given to her by the Calcutta Corporation. Nirmal Hriday grew into 62 centres across the country. The home looked after the poor and the dying. "Nobody there has died feeling unwanted or unloved. We help the poor to die in peace."

Mother was also moved by the plight of lepers. Disowned by their own families, they were forced to beg on the streets. But even the people looked down upon them. This made her establish a home for lepers called Prem Niwas (Home of Love). "Touch a leper, touch him with love," said Mother. She built a leper colony near Asansol called Shanti Nagar (Town of Peace). She explained to the lepers that leprosy was a curable disease and that if they took care of themselves, there would be some improvement in their condition. In Titagarh, she founded the Mahatma Gandhi Leprosy Ashram. She herself brought many of those who suffered from the disease to the ashram.

Besides, Mother was also moved by the plight of newborn or the unborn, who were either abandoned after birth or killed before birth. So she established Nirmal Shishu Bhavan for poor, orphaned and abandoned children. Infants are brought to the home and looked after and nursed by the sisters. As they grow, the children are educated and trained for a profession.

Mother Teresa started her work with just Rs 5. Now the work has expanded to 750 centres in 125 countries. The centres provide education, medical facilities and a home for the poor, destitute and dying. At these centres, everyday around five lakh people are fed and clothed. The centres provide medical relief to about 1.5 lakh sick people and education to more than 20,000 children from slums and poor settlements. Besides, the centres also provide succour to people suffering from AIDS and substance abuse. Mother believed, "to do something beautiful for God is what life is all about".

Through her unflagging work, she commanded universal respect. It was thanks to this respect that she received government and private donations to carry out her work.

In 1964 when Pope Paul VI came to India and presented her with his ceremonial limousine, she immediately raffled it to raise money for her leper colony. In January 1971 she was honoured with the first Pope John XXIII Peace Prize by Pope Paul. The cash award of $21,500 went to the cause of leprosy patients. The cash money that came with the Magsaysay Award went into the construction of a children's home in Agra.

Mother Teresa was a simple lady. She always wore a white saree and had simple living and eating habits. She was awarded the Padma Shri in 1963 and the Nobel Peace Prize in 1979. She was also honoured with the Bharat Ratna, the Leo Tolstoy International Award, the British Order of Merit, the Ceres Medal of the FAO, apart from various other awards, but she claimed that her biggest honour was to work for the poor and the needy. She showed the world that if one had the 'milk of human kindness', one could see God in every human being.

On 5 September 1997 she died in Calcutta. The world mourned her death. India's "saint of the gutters" was buried in the Mother House, the headquarters of the Order of Missionaries of Charity.

Mother once said, "My work is just a drop when what is needed is an ocean of compassion. If I did not put in that one drop, the ocean would be one drop less." But it was French President Jacques Chirac who aptly summed up her contribution: "This evening there is less love, less compassion, less light in the world."

Dr B.R. Ambedkar

Leader of the Dalits

(1891-1956)

Dr Bhimrao Ramji Ambedkar was born into a low caste Mahar family on 14 April 1891 in Mhow, Madhya Pradesh. As society followed a rigid caste system, people of a low caste were considered untouchables. People of the Mahar caste were brave and admitted into the army. Bhimrao's father Ramji Rao also served in the army. When the family migrated to Bombay from their village, Bhimrao was admitted to Elphinston College. They lived in a small tenement where there was not enough space for the whole family, so the father and son slept in turns.

Ambedkar had to face a lot of difficulties in his quest for education. The Maharaja of Baroda helped him and so, after completing his B.A., he went to America for his Master's. He did research on India's economy and obtained his doctorate. After coming back to India, he started practising law in Bombay. Along with his practice, he also worked for the uplift of the socially backward classes. It was this work which drew him close to Gandhiji.

In 1931 when Gandhiji went to London for the Round Table Conference, he accompanied Gandhiji as a representative of the backward classes, while Gandhiji was the representative of the Congress. The Congress was not in favour of giving separate representation to the backward classes. But Ambedkar strongly advocated separate representation for the backward classes. A compromise was reached by the Poona Pact of 1932. The backward classes were given the right to draw water from local wells and ponds and visit temples and other public places. Due to the efforts of Dr Ambedkar, the attitude of society towards these classes changed. But Dr Ambedkar was not happy with the results, so he converted to Buddhism on 14 October 1956.

Ambedkar was accused of creating a rift in Hinduism when he converted to Buddhism. Earlier he had founded the Depressed Classes Association and worked for the amelioration of the suffering of the Dalits or backward classes. In 1947, Pt Nehru included him in his Cabinet as the law minister.

Ambedkar's health deteriorated because of his rigorous work. His wife had died many years ago. In 1948, at the age of 57, he married Lakshmi Savita. She was a doctor and took good care of Ambedkar. He died on 6 December 1956.

In 1990, the man who was the driving force behind the drafting of the Constitution of independent India, Dr Ambedkar was awarded the Bharat Ratna posthumously.

Poets and
Writers

Rabindranath Tagore

Great Poet and Philosopher

(1861–1941)

Gurudev Rabindranath Tagore is one of our country's most distinguished and respected men of letters. Tagore was a novelist, playwright, painter, philosopher, educationist, freedom fighter and an actor. On 13 November 1913, he was awarded the Nobel Prize in Literature for his collection of well-known poems *Gitanjali*.

Tagore also wanted to evolve a world culture, a synthesis of eastern and western values, and towards this end he also founded an international educational institute Shantiniketan at Bolepur in West Bengal in 1901. Shantiniketan later developed into the Vishvabharati University.

Tagore was a voluminous writer. Besides the famous *Gitanjali*, his other well-known poetic works include *Sonar Tari, Puravi, The Cycle of the Spring, The Evening Songs,* and *The Morning Songs*. The names of some of his well-known novels are: *Gora, The Wreck, Raja Rani, Muktadhara, Raj Rishi, Ghare Baire, Nauka Dubi* and *Binodoni. Chitra* is his famous play in verse. *Kabuli Wallah* and *Kshudita Pashan* are two of his famous stories. All of us know that our National Anthem *Jana Gana Mana...* was composed by Tagore.

Rabindranath Tagore was born on 7 May 1861 in Calcutta. His father's name was Devendranath. The British Government honoured him with the title of 'Sir'. But he returned this title in 1919, in protest against the Jallianwala Bagh tragedy.

This great son of India died on 8 August 1941 at the age of 80. One of the last Century's most influential Indian authors, he was also an ardent nationalist who urged social reform.

Sharat Chandra Chatterjee

Litterateur with a Difference

(1876–1938)

The distinction of this famous and highly popular Bengali novelist is that he had the audacity to change the tradition of idealism that was created by Bengali literature. His works centred on the plight and position of women in society. Sharat Chandra Chatterjee was not born into a well-to-do family like Tagore, but with his exceptional flair for writing, he became popular as a great literary figure.

He portrayed the lives and times of people belonging to the lower strata of society who were oppressed, especially the womenfolk of Bengali society. An example of such a work is *Shrikant*. Whatever he wrote, he questioned the very ideals of the Bengali joint family system. He portrayed the society of his times with so much realism and emotion that prominent writers like Romain Rolland recognised him as a literary figure of the first order. That is why he became a popular writer within a short span of time.

Sharat Chandra was born at a village in Hooghly district of West Bengal in 1876. He was the second of nine children. His father had an interest in writing and handicrafts, but he could not pull himself together and work at one place. Sharat Chandra believed that he had inherited his father's 'restless soul'.

Having passed his matric from Bhagalpur, he took admission in Intermediate. But as he was not able to pay his fees on time, he was not allowed to sit for the examination. His mother's death and his father's scolding forced him to run away from home. Having wandered from home, he went to Calcutta and married a girl named Hrinmayi. He soon became a well-known figure in the literary circle of Calcutta. He published his first story in the form of a series in a magazine called *Yamuna*. Then he went to Hooghly and concentrated on his writing.

The female characters in Sharat Chandra's works have an air of mystery surrounding them and cast a spell in the minds of the readers. A few of his popular works are *Badi Didi, Parineeta, Panditji, Samaj ki Atyachaai, Chandranath, Shrikant, Devdas, Charitraheen, Grihadaah, Brahmin ki Beti, Path ki Devedaar, Shesh Prashna, Subhadra* and others. His prominent short stories are *Bindo ka Beta, Chhota Bhai, Ramer Sumati, Manjhili Didi,* etc. Sharat Chandra's works have been translated into almost all Indian languages. Many have also been translated into English.

Sharat Chandra Chatterjee died at the age of 62 after a long illness in Calcutta in 1938. There have been few literary giants in the 20th Century like him.

Premchand

Hindi Novelist and Short Story Writer

(1880–1936)

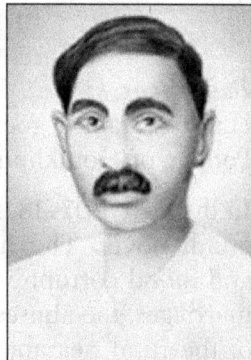

Munshi Premchand wrote in Urdu under his childhood name Dhanpat Rai, but it was when he wrote in Hindi that he became recognised. The one quality of his writing was that he gave a realistic account about the predicament of society. And this made him the *badshah* of Hindi novels.

Premchand was born Dhanpat Rai at Lamahi village in Benares (now Varanasi) on 31 July 1880. His father Ajayab Lal was employed as a clerk in a post office. His mother was Anandi Devi.

Premchand's early education was conducted in Urdu and Persian in Lamahi under the tutelage of a maulvi. He passed his tenth standard from Benares. When he was in the eighth standard, his mother passed away and when he was 15 years old, his father died. Then he had to face a lot of difficulties in life. He was appointed as a teacher at a school in Chunar on a monthly salary of Rs 18. He taught at various schools in Allahabad, Pratapgarh, Kanpur, Gorakhpur and other places. And while he was employed as a school inspector, he completed his graduation. While in Kanpur, he befriended the editor of *Zamana*, Munshi Dayanarayan Nigam, and published his first story in the form of a series in *Zamana*. His work *Prema* was published through Indian Press, Allahabad under the pseudonym 'Nawab Rai'.

The statement that behind every successful man is a woman holds good for Munshi Premchand. His first marriage was not a success. He later married a child-widow Shivani Devi. In spite of facing several hardships, she encouraged her husband to write. Many of his stories were written under the pseudonym 'Nawab Rai'. The first story that was published under his real name was

Bade Ghar ki Beti. The credit of introducing Premchand into Hindi literature goes to Mohan Dwivedi and Mahavir Prasad Poddar of Gorakhpur.

In the year 1917–18, he wrote *Sevasadana.* This was his first major Hindi novel. The novel depicted the problem of prostitution and moral corruption. His works portray the social evils of child marriages, the abuses of the British bureaucracy and exploitation of the rural peasantry by moneylenders and officials.

During that time, he was totally involved in the freedom struggle. He began to churn out articles that focused on social problems. So, he gave up his government job on 15 February 1921 and joined the Marwari school in Kanpur as headmaster.

In 1922, he returned to Benares and founded Saraswati Press. Along with *Gyanmandal,* he started writing for *Madhuri* and *Chand* magazines. The publication of *Rangbhoomi* (1924) exalted him to the status of *badshah* of Hindi novels. *Premashram* (1922), *Karmabhoomi* (1931) and *Godan* (1936) are the other popular works of Premchand. In March 1930, he brought out a magazine called *Hansh* but he was always short of finances.

He went to Bombay in 1935, wrote stories and dialogues for films, but returned to his native place the following year. He breathed his last on 8 October 1936.

'Jigar' Moradabadi

King of Urdu Ghazals

(1890–1960)

'Jigar' Moradabadi is considered to be one of the greatest Urdu poets. He wrote on various subjects and his compositions were simple but profound. His way of rendering poetry was so profound that poets still try to copy his style. He was not highly educated, but overcame these shortcomings.

With dishevelled hair, unshaven beard, bedraggled clothes and an equally intense stupor, before 'Jigar' turned to poetry, he sold spectacles at railway stations. Ali Sikander 'Jigar' Moradabadi was born in 1890 to Maulvi Ali 'Nazar', who was himself an accomplished poet. His father left Delhi and settled in Moradabad. Young 'Jigar' began composing poems at the age of 13. First his father and later 'Daag' Dehalvi, Munshi Amirulla 'Tasleem' and 'Rasa' Rampuri began to help improve his work. The influence of Sufism came into his work through the music of 'Asghar' Gondivi.

He had become an alcoholic, but one day took a solemn pledge not to touch liquor again and stood by it till the very end. But he became ill. Then he took to smoking, but gave it up later and took to playing cards. 'Jigar' Moradabadi had a good sense of humour and was a kind-hearted person. He was also a deeply religious person but kept away from religious fundamentalism. He protested against modernity but was influenced into writing progressive poems.

'Jigar' Moradabadi's first composition *Daag-e-Jigar* was published in 1921, then in 1923 a compilation *Shola-e-Tuur* was published by the Aligarh Muslim University. In 1958, he published *Aatish-e-gul* and the next year he received the Sahitya Akademi Award. On September 1960, the king of Urdu ghazals died in Gonda.

'Josh' Malihabadi

Eminent Revolutionary Poet

(1894–1983)

Thanks to his revolutionary poems, composed during the rule of the British, renowned Urdu poet 'Josh' Malihabadi was given the title *Shayar-e-Inquilab*. He had an incredible form of expression. His words were fiery and could inspire patriotism. After Partition, he moved to Pakistan because of which he was strongly condemned. But his poetry can never be forgotten.

'Josh' Malihabadi was born into a respectable family and had a great deal of sophistication. He was also fearless, brave and sentimental. In the poetry sessions where the audience consisted of Muslim clerics, he sang compositions which condemned them. When the audience comprised government officials, he sang the famous poem *Maatam-e-Azadi* and where women formed the audience, he sang *Hai Jawani, Hai Jawani*. Clergymen despised him, officials shunned him and women walked out in embarrassment, but 'Josh' remained indifferent.

'Josh' had a stout figure and a towering personality and would often mock and poke fun at others. Shabir Hussain Khan 'Josh' was born on 5 December 1894 in the family of a landlord at Malihabad town in Lucknow district, which is famous for mangoes. Even as a child he was temperamental. He would beat up children with a stick. As a youth, he become a fundamentalist and opposed family members. Later he renounced religious fundamentalism.

When the struggle for Independence was on, he became a part of the struggle and composed revolutionary poems. They were published, distributed and read away from public glare.

He went to Hyderabad to earn a livelihood, but could not. He then went to Delhi and started a monthly magazine *Kaleem*. After

Independence, Pt Nehru appointed him the editor of the Urdu edition of the monthly *Aajkal.*

In 1955, he was lured by some Pakistani leaders and shifted base to Pakistan. But the promises made to him were not kept and he lost the respect of the people too. Even in India, people rejected him.

In 1967, he retired and in 1983 he died a dejected man in Islamabad. In his autobiography, *Yaadon ki Baraat,* he praised India and Indian leaders lavishly. So the Pakistan Government confiscated the book. Around a dozen compilations of his poems have been published. How well had he said: "This is the rendition of a heartbroken man."

Harivansh Rai Bachchan

Most Popular Hindi Poet

(1907-2003)

Among Hindi poets, perhaps nobody has gained more popularity than Harivansh Rai Bachchan – and the same popularity has been infused into his son, Amitabh, who has scaled new heights in the film industry. One can see the role of destiny here.

In the 1930s the publication of *Madhushala* saw him soar dizzy heights. In poetry sessions, the audience wished to hear Bachchan alone. With the publication of *Madhushala, Nisha Nimantran, Ekant Sangeet* and other compositions, he established himself as a prominent Indian poet. He began to be compared with other impressionist poets like Sumitranandan Pant, Mahadevi Verma, *et al.* In spite of being introspective, his poems occupy a special place because of the expressions, language and idiomatic phrases.

By writing his autobiography in four volumes, he established himself as a prose writer too. Thanks to his descriptions, his compositions were liked by people, but this caused many a controversy in the literary field.

Harivansh Rai Bachchan was born on 27 November 1907 at Allahabad, Uttar Pradesh. He graduated from the Allahabad University in 1929. It was during this time that he got married. He had completed his first year in MA in English literature when he plunged into the freedom struggle at the call of Gandhiji. For his livelihood, he joined the daily *Pioneer* that was being published from Allahabad. Soon he was appointed a teacher at Agrawal School. Those were testing times because his wife Shyamla was critically ill. In 1936, she died.

He then completed his MA second year. He continued with his poetic compositions and also found recognition. His compositions swept a Sikh teacher, Teji Suri, off her feet and she became attracted towards him. In 1942 they were married. Bachchan was then the lecturer of English at Allahabad University.

His second wife was his muse and infused new inspiration and life into Bachchan. Then his compositions *Halahal, Bengal ka Kal, Milan Yamini, Khadi ke Phool, Pranay Patrika, Aarti aur Angare,* etc. were published. In 1952, he went to Cambridge to carry on research on the Irish poet W.B. Yeats. He returned to India two years later with his doctorate degree. He worked at All India Radio for some time and then moved on to the Foreign Ministry in Delhi as a Special Officer of the Hindi language. Later he was appointed a Member of the Rajya Sabha.

Bachchan's poetic compositions span around three dozen. Besides introspective poems, he composed poetry in the modern technique. He has also translated some of Shakespeare's plays like *Macbeth, Othello, Hamlet,* and *King Lear* into Hindi and received rave reviews. For the translation of *64 Russian Poems,* he received the Soviet Land Nehru Award. He received the Sahitya Akademi Award for *Do Chattanen.* He was also honoured by the Afro-Asian Writers' Conference with the Lotus Award.

Bachchan was an invaluable asset to the literary world. His compositions are simple, which makes it easy for people to remember and hum them. His poems are the poetic depiction of the ancient experiences of the human mind and soul.

Poet Sumitranandan Pant said, "Had it not been for Bachchan, a very important and integral part of *Khari Boli* would have remained uneventful."

He died on 18 January 2003 in Mumbai.

'Agyeya'

Father of Modern Hindi Poetry

(1911–1987)

The credit of giving a modern touch to Hindi literature goes to 'Agyeya'. His poetry, stories and novels have not only established a new style, but have become a benchmark for contemporaries as well as for writers of the new generation. *Shekhar–Ek Jiwani*, published in two volumes, *Nadi ke Dweep* and *Apne-apne Ajnabi* are the only three novels that he wrote, but were enough to gain him recognition. About a dozen of his poems were also published, through which he gave a new direction to literature. The fresh appeal of his compositions was because of his language, expression and subjects.

His name was Sachchidananda Hirananda Vatsyayan. Apart from being a writer, he was also a revolutionary thinker, good editor and educationist and achieved fame in every sphere. He came under the influence of revolutionaries quite early in life. And so, he even spent time in prison. He worked as a bomb expert in Chandra Shekhar Azad's group, because he was the only person in the group with a science background. It was here that a litterateur was born and he wrote *Shekhar–Ek Jiwani*. He handed over the work to his sister while he was in jail. When the novel was published, it created ripples in literary circles. Thus began his literary career.

It was during his imprisonment in the jails of Delhi and Lahore that he began his literary and journalistic career. He worked at a weekly *Sainik* in Agra. Then he moved on to *Vishaal Bharat* in Calcutta. During the Second World War, he joined the army and looked after publicity and public relations. In 1946, he quit his job and took up writing. During this period, he had published a couple of poetry compilations. He adopted a new style of language and expression. He gave the name 'experimentalism' to his work. To bring together other poets of the same genre, he published the works of seven poets in a compilation called *Taar Saptak*. The compilation has found its special place in the literary field. Then he published *Doosra Saptak* and *Teesra Saptak* and much later *Chautha Saptak*.

Apart from writing, 'Agyeya' was also involved in teaching and editing. He was the guest-lecturer at California University and Germany's Heidelberg University. He was the editor of *The Times of India*'s weekly *Dinman* and the Hindi daily *Navbharat Times*. Besides, he also edited the monthlies *Prateek* and *Naya Prateek*. In the political field, he was a supporter of Jayprakash Narayan.

'Agyeya' was honoured with the Bharatiya Gyanpeeth and Sahitya Akademi Awards. He was awarded the Bharat-Bharati posthumously by the Uttar Pradesh Government.

Akhilan

Great Tamil Novelist

(1923–1988)

The greatest of all Tamil novelists PV Akhilandam received India's highest literary award, the Gyanpith Award, for his work *Chittarpave* (*Chitrapriya* in Hindi). He wrote over four dozen books and received the Sahitya Akademi, Soviet Land Nehru and other awards. He took active part in the freedom struggle and went to jail several times. He worked in the postal department and later in All India Radio as a producer.

Apart from writing stories and novels, Akhilan also wrote plays, essays and children's literature. Some of his works have also been made into movies. He wrote against social injustice in society. He led his life the Gandhian way.

The works of Akhilan like *Enge Pogirom* ("Where do we go?"), *Betri Tirunagar* ("Vijaynagar"), *Kayal Vishi, Airimalai* ("Volcano") and *Pavaivillakku* are popular. *Enge Pogirom* depicts the social, economic and political problems of the 6th Century. The protagonist is an educated prostitute. *Betri Tirunagar* and *Kayal Vishi* are historical novels. *Pavaivillakku* is an autobiographical novel.

Umashankar Joshi

Eminent Gujarati Poet

(1911–1989)

There is an extraordinary blend of realism and idealism in the compositions of eminent Gujarati poet Umashankar Joshi. Apart from the Sahitya Akademi Award, he also was honoured with the Gyanpith Award. He was appointed the vice-chancellor of Gujarat University and the chairman of the Sahitya Akademi.

Because of his Gandhian beliefs, he participated in the freedom struggle and was even imprisoned on a few occasions. With the purpose of preserving the ideals of Gandhiji, he composed *Vishwashanti*.

Among his published works, *Gangotri, Nisheeth, Pracheen, Aatithiya, Vasant Varsh, Mahaprasthan* and *Abhigya* are the prominent ones. He also translated *Shakuntalam* and *Uttarramcharit* and other Sanskrit works into Gujarati. He also wrote some plays. During his early life, he also wrote poems in English, but never got them published. He also edited the monthly *Sanskriti*. In 1976, he received the Gyanpith Award for his collection of poems titled *Nisheeth*.

The poet believed, "In the materialistic world when society becomes a target of insensitiveness and love loses its piety, man will find solace in poetry alone."

Salman Rushdie

Controversial Author

(Born 1947)

Salman Rushdie is a controversial English writer of Indian origin. He now resides in England. He has penned many novels. It was his third novel that raked up a lot of controversy. When *Satanic Verses* was published in 1988, Islamic fundamentalists claimed that the novel contained objectionable material that was damaging to the religion of Islam and Prophet Mohammad. Ayatollah Khomeini of Iran issued a fatwa against Rushdie and offered a prize of $6 million to the person who killed Rushdie. Since then, the author has been in hiding in England under the protection of Scotland Yard.

Rushdie continues to write and has written many stories and satirical novels. His other important works are *Midnight's Children* (1981) and *East-West* (1994).

Ahmed Salman Rushdie was born on 19 June 1947 in Bombay (now Mumbai). His father was a prosperous businessman. He studied at Rugby School and the University of Cambridge in England. After acquiring a post-graduate degree in history in 1968, he worked as a copywriter in an advertising agency. His first novel, *Grimus,* appeared in 1975. His second novel was *Midnight's Children.* It was about modern India. The novel earned him critical acclaim and international recognition. *Shame* was published in 1983. It mirrored the political life in Pakistan. It was *Satanic Verses* that created a furore in the Islamic world soon after its release in 1988.

Even while in hiding he continued to write. *Imaginary Homelands* was released in 1991. It is a collection of essays and criticism. *East-West* (1994) is a collection of short stories. Then came *The Moor's Last Sigh* (1995), *The Vintage Book of Indian Writing (1947-1997)* (1997) and *The Ground Beneath Her Feet* (1999).

In early 2000, when writers from the Commonwealth countries were felicitated in New Delhi, Rushdie came to India. When *Satanic Verses* was published and there were widespread protests, India had banned the book. So he appealed to the government to lift the ban on the book.

Salman Rushdie was born in Bombay but has lived abroad for many years now. His ancestral home is located near Solan in Himachal Pradesh.

R.K. Narayan

The Creator of Malgudi

(1906-2001)

Renowned English novelist of international fame, R.K. Narayan was born in Madras in 1906. He had his initial education in Madras (Chennai) and later at Maharaja's College in Mysore. He lived in Mysore, the place which had the most influence on him and was reflected in his novels, till his last years. Narayan travelled extensively. Most of his works, starting from his first novel, *Swami and His Friends* (1935) were set in the fictional town of Malgudi. His novels reflect Indian conditions and life and have a unique identity. Malgudi comes to life in his novel, leaving a feeling that the reader is part of Narayan's fictional place. Many scholars regard him as the greatest Indian writer in English and call him 'the Premchand of South India'.

Narayan started his career as a journalist in Mysore and later took to writing novels. He published numerous novels including *The Guide*, which was made into a Hindi film that went on to become a superhit. Most critics consider *The Guide* to be his magnum opus. It is a great romantic saga of a tourist guide and a dancer who meets him while on a visit to a hill resort with her husband.

He has published numerous novels (*Swami & Friends, The Dark Room, The English Teacher, Mr Sampath, The Financial Expert, Waiting for the Mahatma, The Vendor of Sweets, The Painter of Signs, A Tiger for Malgudi,* and *Talkative Man*); five collections of short stories (*A Horse and Two Goats, An Astrologer's Day, Lawley Road, Malgudi Days,* and *The Grandmother's Tale*); two travel books (*My Dateless Diary* and *The Emerald Route*); four collections of essays (*Next Sunday, Reluctant Guru, A Writer's Nightmare* and *A Story-Teller's World*); a memoir (*My Days*), and some translations of Indian epics and myths (*The Ramayana, The Mahabharata,* and *Gods, Demons and Others*).

In 1980, R.K. Narayan was awarded the A.C. Benson Award by the Royal Society of Literature and was made an Honorary Member of the American Academy and Institute of Arts and Letters. In 1989 he was made a member of the Rajya Sabha. He received the Sahitya Akademi Award for *The Guide* (1958).

R.K. Narayan's full name was Rasipuram Krishnaswami Ayyar Narayanaswami. In his early years he signed his name as R.K. Narayanaswami, but apparently at the time of publication of *Swami and Friends*, he shortened it to R.K. Narayan on Graham Greene's suggestion. He passed away in 2001.

Artists

Raja Ravi Varma

Eminent Artist

(1848–1906)

Raja Ravi Varma acts as a link between the 19th and the 20th centuries. He belonged to a period when Indian art form was trying to break away from the traditional mould and it was Raja Ravi Varma who cast it in the modern mould. His contribution to art is timeless and continues to cast its spell on art lovers even today. That his works still sell at exorbitant rates is proof enough that the charm and attraction of his paintings has not diminished with time. Many of today's painters try to copy his style.

Raja Ravi Varma was born on 29 April 1848 in Kilimanoor, some 36 km away from Trivandrum (now Thiruvananthapuram), the present capital of Kerala. He belonged to the royal family of Travancore. His uncle, Raja Raja Varma, was also a good artist. He taught the basics of painting to Raja Ravi Varma and later introduced him to the Tanjore style of painting. When he was 14, Maharaja Ayilyum Thirunal took him to Travancore and placed him under the tutelage of the royal painter, Rama Swamy Naidu. Three years later he started learning oil painting from a British painter, Theodore Jenson.

Raja Ravi Varma entered the field of art at the dawn of the Modern Age. Of the known artists, he was the first to work with oil. His works were greatly inspired by the European style. Rembrandt was his greatest inspiration, but the subjects of his works remained Indian goddesses and mythological figures. He was the first artist to adopt Western techniques and the principles of perspective and composition in Indian art. In 1873 he won the Governor's Gold Medal for his work *Nair Lady Doing Her Hair*. This made him a popular artist and the Indian nobility and Europeans in the country commissioned him to do their portraits. He did the portraits of the kings of Madras, Trivandrum, Baroda, Udaipur and other states.

He was also the first artist to put his works on display. Art lovers, collectors and many kings and maharajas had the opportunity to buy his works. This gave him an opportunity to move out of Kerala and interact with the people and culture of other parts of the country, and develop a truly national style in his paintings.

The portraits helped him gain instant success, but he moved to painting gods and goddesses from the rich Indian mythology. Some of his works where he captured dramatic and significant moments from Indian mythology include *Shakuntala's Love Letter, Vishwamitra-Menaka, Harishchandra in Distress, Sri Krishna–Balaram, Mohini, Rukmangada, Jatayu Vadha, Sri Rama Vanquishing the Sea* etc. The women depicted in Raja Ravi Varma's works are greatly appreciated. In fact the beauty of the Indian women is sometimes described thus: "She looked as if she had stepped out of a Ravi Varma canvas." It is truly a compliment to the great painter who successfully combined tradition with modernity.

It was in 1893 that his paintings were first exhibited outside Kerala and that too in Delhi. Till then, only kings, princes and the rich had the privilege of visiting a painting exhibition. Ravi Varma's paintings reached the common masses. This was an absolutely commendable achievement in the 20th Century.

To make copies of his originals by the lithography technique, he set up a printing press at a tourist spot in Lonavala in 1894. This resulted in further popularity of Raja Ravi Varma's paintings. His critics, however, condemned his works, pointing out that his paintings were only superficially Indian. They said that though he depicted characters and themes from Indian mythology, he was heavily influenced by Western styles of painting.

Some critics dismiss his works as calendar art, but his oeuvre continues to generate interest among art lovers even now. One of his paintings, *The Begum's Bath* once sold at a record price for an Indian artist.

Nandalal Bose

Great Painter

(1882–1966)

Nandalal Bose is known as the creator of painters because when Rabindranath Tagore brought him to Shantiniketan, he gave Bose the liberty to decide the curriculum of the students of art. As a result, Shantiniketan became a leading institution. It was Nandalal's prudence that was at work. He always tried to help the students get due recognition for their work.

Nandalal Bose was the president of Kala Bhavan of Shantiniketan. He was always concerned with the well-being of his students, so they called him 'Master Moshai'.

Nandalal Bose was born on 3 December 1882 at Munger in Kharagpur, West Bengal. His father worked on a canal project there, but was later transferred to Darbhanga region and appointed the sculptor of a school of architecture. As a child, Nandalal was not very interested in studies. While going to school, he used to watch the potters making clay toys. With the money meant for books and stationery, he bought books devoted to art. At the age of 23, he sought admission in Calcutta Arts School. There he met Abindranath Tagore. In the test Abindranath asked him to draw a picture of Lord Ganesha. Bose drew it with Tempora and watercolours. He passed the test and was taken in as a student.

Bose's paintings were inspired by the paintings of Ajanta and Ellora Caves. In 1910–11, he began to make replicas of the Ajanta paintings. As an instructor at Kala Bhavan, he earned recognition and fame. He accompanied Rabindranath Tagore on his tour to China and Japan in 1924. Among his famous paintings are *Sati*, *Kali*, *Alekshya Dasana*, *Swarna Kalash*, *Ardhnareshwar*, *Veenavadini* and *Parthasarathi*. He died on 16 April 1966.

Amrita Shergil

Maestro of Modern Art

(1913–1941)

A name to reckon with in the art circle, Amrita Shergil painted realistic art and became a well-known figure at a time when European painting was just in the initial stages. Besides she also portrayed Indian rural womenfolk with such natural beauty that her work was well recognised. In her brief life, she created such masterpieces that even decades after her death, her work remains much sought after. She started at a very young age and her work portrayed the talent of an inborn painter.

Amrita Shergil was the daughter of Umrao Singh Shergil of Majitha. She was born in Budapest, the capital city of Hungary. Her mother was a Hungarian. When Umrao Singh went to France, he made arrangements for his daughter's education in Paris. Her uncle, Indologist Ervin Batkay, noticed her talent early and encouraged her to paint. At 16 she entered a famous art school in Paris, Ecole des Beaux Arts. Here she was influenced by the works of Cezanne, Modigliani and Gaugin. The description she heard about India from her relatives invoked a desire to visit the country.

In 1921, she graduated in painting from the city of Florence in Italy. In the test, she painted a nude woman. For this, she was asked to leave the school. She had by this time realised that her sole ambition in life was to become an artist. So she returned to Paris and began to pursue her painting classes again. Soon the influence of Hungarian art in her works began to diminish and her inclination towards realism grew. Her works clearly showed this influence. Her famous paintings include *A Boy with an Apple*, and *Banana Vendor*, among others. The inspiration to paint Indian women came from her fans.

After coming over to India, she opened a studio in Shimla. She transformed herself in the Indian mould and began to paint with the Indian perspective in mind, gaining quick recognition. She wanted to invoke her Indian roots. In 1936, she toured the Ajanta and Ellora Caves and her paintings underwent a transformation. Instead of doing large paintings, she concentrated on doing small, realistic paintings. Thus, she gave a new direction to the Indian art scenario. She tried to fuse the aesthetics of the Ajanta and Ellora paintings with European oil painting techniques that she had learnt in Paris. Her style was a total contrast from the works of contemporaries like Abindranath Tagore, AR Chugtai and Nandalal Bose.

Many of her paintings have a peaceful and soulful expression. But in her own life, she was highly emotional as well as critical and abrasive by nature. Not many readers know that the nude paintings she did depicted reality. In one of her paintings, she portrayed two young girls in the nude, a common sight in rural India.

Her paintings showed diversity after she went on a tour to south India in 1937. This transformation can be seen in many of her works like *Brahmacharis, South Indians Going to the Market* and *Bride's Toilette*. Her work was different from the realist watercolour mode of Indian painting prevalent at the time. This makes it evident that Amrita Shergil's inclination was towards the depiction of modern India rather than being a part of the revival of ancient art that was taught at Shantiniketan.

In 1938 Shergil married a relative from her mother's side, Victor Egan, who was a doctor by profession. She stayed in a small village in northern India. She turned to seventeenth Century Mughal miniatures amalgamating their sense of composition and colour with the system she had developed from Ajanta oil paintings. But her life was cut short by the cruel hands of death. In 1941, at the young age of 28, she died in mysterious circumstances, having already achieved much recognition within a short span of time.

Maqbool Fida Husain

Controversial Contemporary Painter

(1915–2011)

Maqbool Fida Husain was born with a paint-brush in his mouth. He had said, "Even before I had outgrown my childhood, I was told by my father to earn my livelihood. In fact my first paint-brush was given to me by my father. I moved from Indore to Bombay... armed with a paint-brush in my hand and a passion for art... I just followed my passion and went with the flow."

His life was always embroiled in controversies. His works always remained controversial or high profile. He used extremely long brushes and paints. He was never embarrassed to exhibit his weakness for the fairer sex and was a great fan of Madhuri Dixit.

As per Husain, "I was not even two years old when I lost my mother. Maybe that is why my search for a mother figure is eternal... maybe that is the reason why, in most of my paintings, I never show faces. When I wanted to depict the affection of a mother, I painted Mother Teresa... the moment people saw that white saree with the blue border, they just knew it was Mother."

At one time he painted horses in full gallop. Could it be that the horses were symbolic of his restless and roving heart and mind? Apart from painting scenes from the *Ramayana* and the *Mahabharata* he had also drawn portraits of Mahatma Gandhi, Mother Teresa, Indira Gandhi, Amitabh Bachchan, Madhuri Dixit and Sachin Tendulkar. All these prove that an artist is always on the lookout for something new. He conducted his daughter's marriage ceremony in a chawl of a Mumbai suburb called Girgaon.

M.F. Husain was nominated to the Rajya Sabha for six years. He tried to portray society in his work. M.F. Husain was born on 17 September 1915 at Pandharpur in Maharashtra. After completing his initial studies in 1935 in Indore, he came over to Bombay to join the J.J. School of Arts. He began his career by painting cinema posters on hoardings. However, the money he earned was not enough to support him and his wife, Fazila, whom he married in 1941. Though he also tried his hand at designing toys and furniture, painting was his first love. He put up his first painting on display at the Bombay Art Society in 1947. It was titled *Sunhera Sansar*.

In 1948 on the invitation of the painter Francis Newton Souza, he became a member of the Progressive Artists Group. The group aimed at giving a natural expression to contemporary Indian art. There he was influenced by the German painter Emile Nolde and the Austrian Oscar Kokoschka, who were renowned painters of the Expressionist tradition. He was influenced by their style. In the 1950s he held solo exhibitions first in Zurich and later in Europe and the United States.

He joined hands with modernist architect Balkrishna V. Doshi and created the Husain-Doshi Gufa in Ahmedabad. It is a cave-like structure that knits diverse disciplines of art and architecture.

Husain was always inspired by cinema. His first work as a filmmaker was *Through the Eyes of a Painter*. It won the Golden Bear at the Berlin Film Festival in 1967. He depicted scenes from films like *Pather Panchali* and *Hum Aapke Hain Kaun*.

For his contribution towards art Husain was honoured with the Padma Shri in 1966, the Padma Bhushan in 1973 and the Padma Vibhushan in 1989.

Husain was indifferent to religion and politics and treated Hindu Gods & Goddesses with disdain depicting them unclothed and often in sexuality suggesting poses. This led to a series of cases as well as non-bailable warrant against him. Fearing for life, Husain left India in 2006 and lived in London & Doha. He acquired Qatari nationality. He expired on 9 June 2011.

M.S. Subbulakshmi

Melody Queen

(1916–2004)

Madurai Shanmugavadivu Subbulakshmi has the distinction of making it big in the field of Carnatic music when it was strictly a male domain. MS, as she is popularly called, was born in the temple town of Madurai, Tamil Nadu on 16 September 1916. Her mother Madurai Shanmugavadivu was an exceptional veena player. Young Subbulakshmi (the name means 'the auspicious goddess of wealth') grew up listening to the notes of the nagaswaram and the chants emanating from the Meenakshi Temple near her house. She dropped out of school when she was in the fourth standard and dedicated herself to music. Her guru was Semmangudi Srinivasa Iyer. Subbulakshmi was a child prodigy. She gave her first recital in 1926 when she was just 10 years old. She has continued to enthrall audiences since then.

In the field of music, India has produced many eminent musicians. And each occupies a special place in the music world. But what is it that puts MS Subbulakshmi apart? The answer is that as soon as she sets her hands on the mridangam, she forgets herself and words flow from her mouth and resonate in the air. The grace and dedication with which she sings has resulted in a huge fan following. She always wants her audience to be immersed in music and feel a divine presence.

In 1938, Subbulakshmi made her film debut with *Sevasadanam*. It was based on the theme of women's liberation. In 1940, she married Thyagarajan Sadasivam, a freedom fighter, who was also her guru and guide. A major credit for Subbulakshmi's success goes to her husband, who shaped her musical career. Sadasivam was also a filmmaker. Subbulakshmi appeared in Tamil films as a singing star, all of which were runaway successes. She acted in *Shakuntalai* in 1940, *Savitri* in 1941 and *Meera* in 1945. *Meera* was remade in Hindi and became a hit. The film made her a household name across the country.

However, it was her devotional songs (*bhajans* and *shlokas*) that made her truly famous in India and abroad. She has rendered her voice to the compositions of the Carnatic music trinity – Thyagaraja, Muthuswamy Dikshitar and Shyama Sastri. When she sang Gandhiji's favourite bhajan *Vaishnava Janato Tene Kahiye, Je Peer Parayee Jaane Re*, magic was created on stage and he was moved to tears. Amongst her famous renditions are *Shree Venkatesha Suprabhatam, Shree Vishnu Sahasranaman, Meera bhajans* and *Hanuman Chalisa.*

When MS sang at the United Nations Assembly, *New York Times* wrote that she could convey her message to Western people through her music. Although they could not understand the words, the sweet voice emanating from her throat made the message easy to grasp for foreigners. She also sang before the Queen of England at Royal Albert Hall in London.

When Sarojini Naidu heard her renditions, she said, "From today, I surrender to Subbulakshmi, the enchanting singer with an enchanting voice, my title (the Nightingale of India)."

In 1954 Subbulakshmi was honoured with the Padma Bhushan. She received the title of Sangeetha Kalanidhi in 1969. She was the first woman to be honoured by the Madras Music Academy. In 1974, she received the Magsaysay Award and the following year she received the Padma Vibhushan. She was the recipient of the Indira Gandhi Award for national integration in 1990. She was honoured with the Bharat Ratna in 1998, the first musician to be honoured with this award. She created a great void when her soul left for her heavenly abode on December 11, 2004.

Lata Mangeshkar

Greatest Female Playback Singer

(Born 1929)

There are a number of well-known playback singers in the music industry, but by rendering her voice to playback singing for film actresses, Lata Mangeshkar has not only helped them in finding a place of honour for themselves, but has also carved a niche for herself in the world of music.

Lata was the eldest child in a family of four girls – Lata, Asha, Usha and Meena and a brother, Hridaynath. Her father Dinanath Mangeshkar died when she was very young. She entered the film industry as a playback singer at the age of 13 in Marathi films. Nobody could have guessed then that the girl would go on to earn a name for herself and her family in Hindi playback singing.

On one occasion, she met Dilip Kumar. He told her that though a Marathi singer, she should pay attention to her diction in Hindi and Urdu too. And it did not take her long to establish herself.

The secret of her success is that she understands the story line of the film for which she has to playback. Then she studies the temperament of the heroine for whom she has to render her voice. When the film is screened, it seems that the heroine herself is doing the playback, not Lata Mangeshkar.

At a function when Lata sang the composition *Ae mere watan ke logon, zara aankh mein bharlo paani* by Pradeep for an audience that included prominent leaders like Pt Nehru, it brought tears to his eyes.

She has sung over 50,000 songs in 20 Indian languages for thre generations of heroines. This nightingale's velvety voice will continue to resonate for centuries to come. She had received the Dada Saheb Phalke Award in 1989. She was honoured with the Bharat Ratna in 2001.

Vallathol Narayan Menon

Poet & Patron of Kathakali & Mohiniattam

(1858–1958)

Vallathol Narayan Menon was an eminent Malayali poet. He is held in great reverence for his beautiful compositions. In recognition of his poetic talents, the British Government honoured him with an award in literature in 1923, but he displayed immense patriotism by refusing the award. The British Government was taken aback and insulted him by calling him a 'shameless Indian poet'. But this did not have any effect on the poet and he began his work with renewed vigour and vitality. He gave shape to various facets of the freedom struggle through his poetry. He believed it was necessary to keep a record of the past to help India on the path to progress. He felt it was difficult to sever ties with the past before proceeding towards the future.

His perception was very extensive. The contribution of Bala Saraswati, Rukmini Devi, MS Subbulakshmi, Ravi Shankar, Vallathol etc. towards art indicates a period of Renaissance of Indian art and literature. Apart from writing poetry, he also patronised Kathakali and Mohiniattam dance forms of Kerala. He set up the Kerala Kala Mandalam for the promotion of these dance forms. He toured the country and also went abroad.

Today both Kathakali and Mohiniattam have been given the status of classical dance.

Kamladevi Chattopadhyay

Reviver of Folk Arts

(1903–1988)

What is significant about Kamladevi Chattopadhyay is that she has made a contribution towards every field of art. Till Independence, Indian handicrafts were discouraged. Kamladevi organised the handicrafts sector, gave it the much-needed stability and tried to boost it. Her contribution towards handicrafts, music, theatre and dance is immense and incomparable.

Apart from handicrafts, ancient art forms like folk theatre, painting and singing have come down as part of our heritage. Due to colonisation by the British, proper attention was not paid to the ancient art forms and their survival was in peril. Another problem was the backwardness of rural women. In spite of being involved in handicrafts and folk art, their economic condition was very poor. When Kamladevi became a member of the women's wing of the All-India Congress Committee, she took important steps to improve the condition of womenfolk, though she herself was fighting heavy odds on the personal front.

She was married at a very young age and soon became a child widow. If she hadn't received the support of her mother and maternal grandmother, she would have ended up in a pitiable condition as hundreds of child widows did during that age. They were determined to give her higher education. She soon came in contact with Harindranath Chattopadhyay, brother of Sarojini, and showed interest in theatre. He wanted to marry Kamla, but he had to convince her and her mother. Kamladevi married on the condition that she be allowed to continue with her studies. Harindranath was able to instil a new lease of life in her.

Soon she began her work and strived not only to improve the lot of womenfolk, but society as a whole. She became an exponent of different forms of art and established a number of institutions for art and music. She was also the president of the Sangeet Natak Academy, and the vice president of the Indian Theatre Association and the Asian Theatre Institution. She was also the founder-member of the Handicrafts Board.

She started a number of training centres to provide special training for handicrafts. She also made provisions to sell the products made at these centres. It was because of her fine perception that the Central Cottage Industries could be established.

In the mid-50s, she was a symbol of art. She tried to give an artistic touch to Indian social life. Her contribution towards the field of handicrafts and Indian social life will never be forgotten. She received the Magsaysay Award in 1966.

Pt. Ravi Shankar

Renowned Sitarist

(Born 1920)

The contribution of Pt Ravi Shankar to the field of music will be remembered forever. There is no doubt that he plays magic on the sitar and has made instrumental music popular across the world. And that is what makes him incomparable. He has helped classical music and the sitar gain worldwide recognition.

It is because of his music that he is considered a world citizen. His students belong to different countries. Despite fame, he has never changed. He always wears a kurta-pyjama.

Pt Ravi Shankar developed the notation technique for teaching the sitar to his students. He has developed new tunes like _Parmeshwari, Kameshwari, Gangeshwari, Jogeshwari, Vairag Todi, Kaushiktodi, Mohankaunc Rasiya, Manmanjari, Pancham_ etc. His compositions like _Vairagi_ and _Natbhairav_ are quite popular. It was Pt Ravi Shankar who composed the tune of _Sare Jahan Se Achcha_, and that too at the age of 25.

Pt Ravi Shankar was born in Benares (now Varanasi) on 7 April 1920. His elder brother Uday Shankar was a well-known dancer. Ravi Shankar toured the world along with Uday Shankar's dance troupe. He choreographed dance before taking to the sitar. At the age 18 he gave up dance.

For the next seven years he dedicated himself to gain command over the sitar. His guru was Allauddin Khan Saheb of Maihar. He worked as music director at the All India Radio from 1948 to 1956. Then he began to pursue his passion and undertook a series of European and American tours. He introduced Indian music to the west. George Harrison of the Beatles took up learning the sitar from him. Ravi Shankar has performed with renowned musicians and music conductors like violinist Yehudi Menuhin and symphony conductor Zubin Mehta. He even performed *jugalbandis* (duets) with tabla player Ustad Allah Rakha and sarod player Ali Akbar Khan.

Shankar composed a number of film songs like Satyajit Ray's Apu trilogy, *Meera, Godaan* and *Anuradha.* He composed *Raaga Swarna* on the occasion of the 50th anniversary of India's independence. In 1969 his autobiography *My Life, My Music* was published.

In a career spanning more than six decades, Ravi Shankar has been honoured with a number of awards. Various universities from India and abroad have honoured him with around 14 doctorates. He received the Padma Bhushan (1967), two Grammy awards (1966 and 1972), Padma Vibhushan (1981), the Magsaysay Award (1992), the Polar Music Prize (1998), Japan's Praemium Imperiale Award "for encouraging efforts of future generations of artistes", the Bharat Ratna (1999) and France's highest civilian award, Commandeur de La Legion d'Honneur (2000).

Rukmini Devi Arundale

Bharat Natyam Exponent

(1904–1986)

Rukmini Devi Arundale made an indispensable contribution towards art and culture. She is chiefly remembered for three prominent contributions in the field of art. Her marriage to George Arundale drew her close to ballet. It was then that renowned Russian ballerina Anna Pavlova advised her to find inspiration in the Indian art form.

Soon she was inclined towards Bharat Natyam. Till then this art form was practised only by the *Devadasis* – temple dancers who were looked down upon by high society. This ancient dance form was on the verge of decline. Then founder-member of the Madras Music Academy, E. Krishna Iyer inspired Rukmini Devi to take up the dance form. With the help of some motivated *devadasis*, she revived the declining art form. She gave Bharat Natyam a modern form by giving it a dress code, accessories and make-up, thereby imparting a permanent form to the dance. The worldwide recognition that Bharat Natyam has received is due to Rukmini Devi.

Though she belonged to a high-class Brahmin family, she learnt to perform on stage, inspiring ladies from a good family background to learn this dance form.

Another significant work of hers was the formation of Kalakshetra. The institution was run on the teacher-pupil tradition of ancient India. Art was being carried out through the centuries based on this tradition. Kalakshetra was established for the propagation of art and literature among the people and many famous artists and musicians have been associated with it.

She also started the tradition of musical dance ballets. She thus gave a modern touch to traditional dance and her contribution towards arts and culture will be remembered for ages to come.

Philosophers and
Thinkers

Dr S. Radhakrishnan

Philosopher, Scholar and Statesman

(1888–1975)

Dr Sarvepalli Radhakrishnan is regarded as a unique amalgamation of an eminent philosopher and a national political leader. His interpretation of Indian philosophy in English has made people in the West change their perception about India. Dr Radhakrishnan is one of the few eminent personalities who had had a truly Indian upbringing and education. And he was able to make a mark in the Indian political, administrative, educational and spiritual spheres.

Dr Radhakrishnan was born on 5 September 1888 at Tiruttani, Tamil Nadu. His father, Veeraswami, was an astrologer and teacher. Dr Radhakrishnan received his early education from his father. He joined Christian College of Madras for his higher education. The one advantage he had of studying in a convent was that he got the opportunity to ponder over the Hindu religion. This was because the Hindu religion was criticised by missionaries. And this filled him with the desire to understand the true essence of Hinduism.

The speeches of Swami Vivekananda inspired him a lot. And that is why he did his post-graduation in philosophy. Then he worked at Presidency College, Madras till 1917. During those times, Dr Visvesvaraya was the diwan of Mysore. So at the behest of Dr Visvesvaraya, he joined Mysore College as a professor of philosophy. In spite of the presence of stalwarts like Dr Radhakumud Mukherjee and Professor Wadia, Dr Radhakrishnan became a popular figure in the university.

Dr Radhakrishnan did not obtain a doctorate degree. It was because of his competence, writing skills and insight into philosophy that many universities awarded him doctorate degrees. Just as Dr Visvesvaraya was keen to make Mysore an ideal state,

Sir Ashutosh Mukherjee wanted to promote Calcutta as a centre of science and education. So he invited Dr Radhakrishnan to Calcutta.

It was during this time that Andhra University was founded and he was appointed the vice-chancellor. He also had to look into the administration and organisation of the University. Although he joined Andhra University, he did not sever ties with Calcutta University. He was also given the financial charge of Andhra University. When he was in Calcutta, he was also associated with Oxford University, England. So he spent six months of a year in Calcutta and the other half in England. During those days, Madan Mohan Malaviya established Benares Hindu University and wanted to appoint Dr Radhakrishnan as the vice-chancellor of the University. Dr Radhakrishnan agreed to join as vice-chancellor but refused to work on a salary. In this way, he worked in Calcutta, Benares and Oxford Universities simultaneously. But when the work of Benares University required more of his involvement, he bade farewell to Calcutta University.

In 1942, when the freedom struggle took a new turn, the students of Benares University joined it. The British Government wanted to close the University. Because the students were also in favour of this, it would not have been difficult for the British to do so. But Dr Radhakrishnan was not in favour. Many considered this act of his unpatriotic, but it was not so. The institution founded by Madan Mohan Malaviya was a nationalist one.

Dr Radhakrishnan spent 40 years of his life as an educationist. Apart from being a teacher, he was also a writer, administrator and politician. His contribution as a teacher and educationist was noticed in Oxford, Calcutta and Benares Hindu Universities. Later, he was appointed the ambassador to the Soviet Union. And he was good at his work. It is said that when Dr Radhakrishnan completed his tenure as the ambassador and was taking leave from the dictator, Josef Stalin remarked, "You are the first person who treated me as a human being and not as a ghost. I am saddened by the fact that you are leaving us. I may not live long, but I wish you a long life." So saying, the mighty leader's eyes welled up with tears.

The diplomatic handling of the relationship between the two countries by Dr Radhakrishnan helped build friendly ties in the formative years of India's existence. What augmented the relationship was his humanitarian thought, simplicity and humanity.

When Dr Radhakrishnan returned to India in 1952, he was elected the vice-president. Between 1953 and 1962, he also served as the vice-chancellor of the University of Delhi.

On 11 May 1962, he succeeded Dr Rajendra Prasad as the President. The world welcomed his presidency. He always upheld the glory and honour of every post that he held. Be it as the Professor of Eastern Religions and Ethics at Oxford University between 1936 and 1952 or as the chairman of the United Nations Educational, Scientific and Cultural Organisation (UNESCO) between 1946 and 1952.

Dr Radhakrishnan was simple to the core. He always wore a *dhoti*, a *bandgala* coat and a turban. He tried to interpret Indian thought and philosophy for Westerners. His works include *Indian Philosophy, The Philosophy of the Upanishads, The Hindu View of Life, Eastern Religion and Western Thought* and *East and West: Some Reflections.*

Jiddu Krishnamurthi

Great Spiritual Thinker and Philosopher

(1895–1986)

Jiddu Krishnamurthi was born into a Tamilian Brahmin family on 11 May 1895 in Madanapalle, Tamil Nadu. His father was a government officer and when he moved on to Madras, he began to work for the Theosophical Society there. This was how the philosophy of the Theosophists influenced young Krishnamurthi. Seeing the exceptional qualities of the small boy, Annie Besant, the president of the Theosophical Society, proclaimed him as the incarnation of Christ in the west and the Buddha in the east. She took him under her wing and sent him to England, grooming him for his future role as the next world teacher. In 1911, an organisation called 'The Order of the Star in the East' was formed and young Krishnamurthi was appointed its head.

He spread the philosophy of the organisation around the world. He soon became world renowned and was accepted as one of the famous thinkers and philosophers of India. However, in 1922, he experienced a transformation in his ideologies. He questioned the basis of all philosophies and ideologies. In 1929, he dissolved the Order and returned all the money and property he received for his work.

Then he formulated a new philosophy after breaking away from the Theosophical Society. Krishnamurthi was a good orator and in a historic speech, he said, "I maintain that Truth is a pathless land and you cannot approach it through any path whatsoever, by any religion, by any sect." He believed that every person should strive to seek the Absolute Truth by himself. His teaching was: "You are the world and the world is from you."

Krishnamurthi travelled around the world and spread his thoughts to the people. He did not believe in any religion, philosophy or ideology. He believed that man could alleviate his sufferings only if he was determined to do so himself. He also believed that no religion, religious leader or guru could help in ameliorating the sufferings of mankind. It was for man to look inside and rid himself of fears.

He postulated, "To follow another in spiritual matters is to destroy oneself." He maintained that man should have a scientific bent of mind that is triggered by the religious spirit. And for this, man should have the right education.

After the death of Annie Besant, his association with the Theosophical Society was completely severed. Then he settled at California in the US. He died on 17 February 1986 in Ojai, California. A number of schools, beginning with the Rishi Valley School in 1928, were founded in India and abroad, especially in England and the US, based on Krishnamurthi's teachings.

Swami Chinmayananda

Spiritual Thinker

(1916–1993)

Swami Chinmayananda devoted his life to the spread of religious teachings of the sacred Indian texts, especially the *Bhagavad Gita*, the *Upanishads* and the *Vedas*. He also wrote around 30 books that attempt to interpret the dilemmas of the Hindu religion.

Swami Chinmayananda was born Balakrishna Menon on 8 May 1916 in Ernakulam, Kerala. He was born into an aristrocratic family of Kerala. After completing his school education in Kerala, he joined the Lucknow University for his Masters in English literature and law. In 1942, he took part in the freedom struggle and spent many months in jail.

After his graduation he joined *National Herald* in Delhi and wrote on varied subjects. Though he was successful in his profession, he was quite dissatisfied. The question of life and death and the futility of life and the role of spirituality haunted him.

It was then that he embarked on the quest for his answers. He undertook an extensive study of European and Indian philosophy. He was inspired by the writings of Swami Sivananda. In 1949 he became an ascetic and joined Swami Sivananda's ashram. He took the name Swami Chinmayananda Saraswati meaning 'the one who revels in the bliss of Pure Consciousness'. Under the tutelage of the Vedanta master Swami Tapovan, he studied the ancient Scriptures. He spent eight years here. It was then that it dawned on him that he should get across the message of the Vedanta to the people and bring about spiritual awakening in the country.

He conducted his first religious discourse (*jnana yagna*) in Pune. He soon carried it to prominent cities. The Brahmins (priestly class) were displeased by Swami Chinmayananda's method of open dissemination of the sacred knowledge of the Holy Scriptures. Till then the knowledge was restricted only to the Brahmins. Swami Chinmayananda put across the message of the Vedanta in a simple way that was easy for the common man to understand. He said that the Vedanta proposed to make man happier and contented in his daily life, leading to spiritual awakening from within.

He founded the Chinmaya Mission and preached the holy Indian texts. Every year he held a *Gyan Yagna* in one of the metropolitan cities. Apart from this, he also participated in social services and the spread of education and culture.

In September 1993 he went to Chicago to represent the Hindu religion at the Parliament of World Religions. He was the second Indian after Swami Vivekanand to be given the honour. He, however, suffered a massive heart attack and went into *mahasamadhi* in San Diego, California.

Swami Chinmayananda spent his life like a hermit of ancient India. Because of his selflessness and resoluteness, he was able to make the ancient Indian texts clearer and easy to understand.

Osho Rajneesh

Philosopher and Guru

(1932–1990)

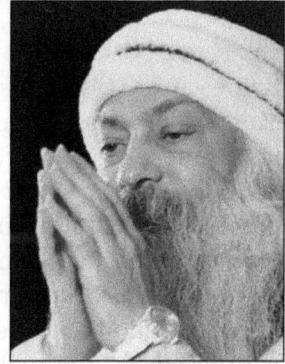

India is the home of many saints, philosophers and spiritual leaders. Many of them still influence society long after they are no more. Osho Rajneesh was one spiritual leader who tried to combine the thoughts and perceptions of Plato to early Chinese thinkers and modern philosophers. Rajneesh remained a controversial religious leader all his life, but there are thousands of his followers around the world.

The thoughts and lifestyle of Rajneesh were totally different vis-a-vis other spiritual leaders from India or abroad. Such people spend their life in meditation and in practising abstinence. But the ashrams and prayer halls of Rajneesh were no less than a modern discotheque. The more you unravel facts about him, the more amazing he seems. His spiritual world was established in the form of a discotheque-like ashram, a publications division, food larder and bakeries, all worth millions. The environment of his prayer halls was contrary to Indian culture. Rajneesh believed that man could achieve salvation only if he first got rid of his carnal desires and then concentrated on spiritualism. In his ashrams men and women were free to interact.

Even after examining his life and his spiritualism in retrospect, it is still not clear if he wanted to start a new faith or not. He has over 600 published books to spread his thoughts among the people and advocated a different method for the concentration of the mind, which is still followed by his followers. Rajneesh was severely criticised for his thoughts on sex and marriage. As a matter of fact, his life itself was surrounded by controversies. Yet he had over 500 prayer houses and meditation centres across the globe and they are still visited by his followers who meditate according to his interpretation of spiritualism.

Rajneesh or 'Osho', as he was later called, was born Chandra Mohan Jain at a village in Madhya Pradesh into the family of a Jain trader. After his education, he was appointed as a lecturer of philosophy at Jabalpur University. In 1966, he left his job and began to preach his thoughts. In 1970, he left for Bombay. There too he started preaching his thoughts in the evenings. Soon the number of his followers increased. Then he started a new form of renunciation and it soon became an international movement. He started his work with just six disciples. His objective was to transform his thoughts into an international one. In 1974, he came to Poona and established an ashram. Even after his death, the ashram continues to draw visitors and tourists. They come here to witness a unique phenomenon of prayer and devotion.

In India he was severely criticised for his thoughts and actions and so he went to America. There he bought 64,000 acres of land in Oregon and founded a city which was named Rajneeshpuram. The work in the city was carried out very fast. People were so influenced by his words that they donated their valuable possessions like Rolls Royce cars etc.

When the American Government perceived the emergence of a special type of culture which was in violation of immigration laws, it asked him to leave the country. Then he returned to Poona and died sometime later at the age of 58.

A controversial spiritual leader of the 20th Century, Osho has many followers in India and abroad. His thoughts and movement are kept alive by his disciples.

Sri Aurobindo

Prominent Revolutionary and Ascetic

(1872–1950)

There are some persons who act as a bridge between two periods, but there are some who cannot be bound within a period and leave their impression on the sands of time forever. The life of Sri Aurobindo is an example of such a person. Wherever he went, he left an indelible mark. His works and philosophy have not only inspired Indians but also the world.

It is sheer coincidence that he was born on 15 August 1872, the same day India gained independence some 75 years later. On the occasion of his 75th birthday, he gave a message which formed the dream of his life:

- There will be a period of renaissance in Asia and Asia will again act as a guiding light for human civilisation.

- India will be a spiritual guide for the rest of the world.

- There will be progress towards man's ultimate development and he will become capable of solving his problems himself.

Aurobindo Ghosh was the third son of Dr K.D. Ghosh and Swarnlata Devi. Influenced by Western culture, his father converted to Christianity. He had studied in England, so he sent his three sons to study at Loretto Convent in Darjeeling for their primary education. After two years, the father went to England and left his children at Manchester, where they studied at St Paul's School. Here Aurobindo studied English, French and Latin. At the age of 10, Aurobindo wrote poetry, which was published in *Fax Family Magazine*. Aurobindo took admission in King's College at Cambridge and also cleared the written examination of the Junior Civil Services, scoring highest marks in Latin and French.

A group of Indian students had formed a secret organisation called 'Lotus and Dagger' that worked clandestinely for the Indian freedom struggle. Aurobindo became a member of the organisation. He gave fiery speeches and recited patriotic songs at the congregation of Indian students called Indian Majlis in Cambridge. It was during these days that Maharaja Sayajirao of Baroda went to London and invited him to work in his kingdom. In 1893, he went to Baroda. His father died the same year. Aurobindo taught English and French to the maharaja. Later he became the principal of Maharaja College at Baroda.

After nearly 14 years in Baroda, he went to Calcutta in 1905, when Lord Curzon partitioned Bengal. Between 1902 and 1910 he strived vehemently to free the country from British rule. He made revolutionary ideas known to the people. He disagreed with the Congress policy of sending petitions and strongly supported the extremist wing of the Congress led by Bal Gangadhar Tilak. His association with the Congress in Calcutta for five years gave a lease of life to the party and it began to penetrate the grassroots level. But God had willed otherwise.

In 1910, when he went to prison, it dawned on him that his area of work lay elsewhere. Listening to the voice of his conscience and God, he forayed onto the path of spiritualism – which he considered the original gift of India to the world.

The British Government considered him a revolutionary. So to get away from the clutches of the British and to carry out his work without any obstacles, he went to the French colony of Chandranagar before moving on to Pondicherry, where he established an ashram for meditation and stayed there for the rest of his life.

According to Aurobindo, freeing man from the bonds of individuality would help mankind achieve *moksha* (salvation). He tried to bring about the union of different spiritual streams. He established a number of ashrams and founded Auroville along with a French lady Mira Richard, later known as 'the Mother'. Auroville is not just an ashram, it is a self-sufficient township, where people from all walks of life and different countries get a new life and work for the progress and betterment of mankind. Aurobindo died on 5 December 1950.

Film Personalities

Dadasaheb Phalke

Father of Indian Films

(1870–1944)

The Indian film industry is the biggest in the world. The number of films churned out by the Indian film industry in a year surpasses even that of Hollywood. Do you know who laid the foundation of the Indian film industry? It was all because of the earnest efforts of Dhundiraj Govind Phalke, fondly called Dadasaheb Phalke. He was inspired to make films when he saw a film on Christ. He dreamt of producing movies on Hindu gods and goddesses. And the realisation of that dream led to the formation of the world's largest film industry.

Dadasaheb Phalke was born on 30 April 1870 in Trymbakeshwar, Maharashtra. Even as a child he showed an inclination towards the creative arts. In 1885, he joined J.J. School of Arts in Bombay. He had varied interests. He worked briefly as a painter, a theatrical set designer and as a photographer in the State Archaeology Department. It was when he had an opportunity to work in the lithography press of celebrated painter Raja Ravi Varma that he was influenced by Varma's paintings of gods and goddesses.

In 1908, he set up Phalke's Art Printing and Engraving Works through a partnership. When it failed, it became difficult for him to make both ends meet. He also had to support his wife and children. It was during those difficult times that he saw the movie, *The Life of Christ* (1910) and his thinking and life took a dramatic turn. This happened during the Christmas of 1911, when he did not have the money or the knowledge about film-making. He arranged for the money by parting with his wife's jewellery, and made the trick film *Birth of a Pea Plant.* For this film, Phalke shot one frame a day to show the plant growing. He showed the film to Yashwant Nadkarni, a photographic equipment dealer, who was amazed by it and agreed to back Phalke. With this money, Phalke opened the Phalke Film Company.

All this took three years and in 1913 he made the film *Raja Harishchandra*. It was written, directed, produced and distributed by him. It is difficult to estimate the trials and tribulations he faced during the making of films. He learnt stage setting, photography, rules of theatre and even magic and illusion. He also mastered painting of the sets and designing as well as learnt the nuances of film distribution. This was indeed a pioneering effort!

In 1917, Phalke Film Company became Hindustan Film Company. He made around 40 films. At a time when films were considered taboo for women, he introduced an actress in the film *Bhasmasur Mohini* (1913). His other successful films include *Lanka Dahan* (1917), *Krishna Janma* (1918) and *Sairandari* (1920). In the 1930s when sound was introduced in Hindi cinema and the film industry expanded, he lost out. So he gave up film-making.

It was 25 years since *Raja Harishchandra* was made. When the Indian film industry was celebrating its silver jubilee, it failed to honour Dadasaheb Phalke. So he died a poor, embittered man on 16 February 1944 at Nasik. The Dadasaheb Phalke Award was constituted a year after his death by the government in recognition of his contribution to the Indian film industry.

Today getting the Dadasaheb Phalke Award for lifetime achievement is a matter of pride and honour for film producers, directors and actors. It is given by no less a personage than the President of India.

Madhubala

Enigmatic Beauty and Legendary Actress

(1933–1969)

Madhubala performed her roles with such flair and finesse that she always looked natural on screen. And this was what people liked about her. Even after the lapse of decades, her movies evoke the same response among the audience of today. She was a combination of beauty, grace and charm.

Madhubala's life was not a happy one. Madhubala's role in *Mughal-e-Azam* was highly appreciated. The character she portrayed in the film was similar to her plight in real life. She came from a poor family and the grace with which she faced the trials and tribulations of her life was similar to the ones faced by the heroine of the movie. She fell in love with her co-actor, Dilip Kumar and wanted to marry him. But her father was against the relationship because he would lose a goose that laid golden eggs. If she were to get married, there was none to take care of her 11 siblings.

At first it was difficult for Madhubala to secure permission to act in films. She came from an orthodox, conservative Muslim family and her father, Ataullah Khan, did not agree initially to let his beautiful daughter act in films. But Madhubala remained steadfast and her father had to give in because he had no other means of sustenance.

Her film career spanned just two decades from 1942 to 1962. She died at the age of 36, leaving behind a void which can never be filled. She started off as a child artist. Then she became a full-fledged actress and heroine with the film *Neelkamal* opposite Raj Kapoor. And then came *Amar, Mr and Mrs 55, Chalti Ka Naam Gaadi, Howrah Bridge, Kaalapani, Mahal, Mughal-e-Azam,* and others. In *Mahal,* she enchants us with the song *Aayega Aanewala,* in *Chalti Ka Naam Gaadi*, she charms us with her cherubic smile and grace as Kishore Kumar tries to persuade her to pay the fees of *Paanch Rupaiya Baarah Anna*, and she is at her best when she portrays herself as a desperate and defiant lover as she renders *Pyaar Kiya to Darna Kya* in *Mughal-e-Azam*.

She faced the vicissitudes of life with a smile on her face. Although she encountered a lot of agony and pain, she never reflected the same in her movies. She did her role in comedy movies like *Chalti Ka Naam Gaadi*, *Half Ticket* and *Mr and Mrs 55* with great poise and ease.

Madhubala is often compared with Marilyn Monroe of Hollywood. Both had great sex appeal, beauty, charm, and enigma. Both led unhappy lives and yearned for love. Both died young.

When she was denied permission to marry Dilip Kumar, she was heartbroken. Finally she married Kishore Kumar, but their marital life was cut short because of her untimely demise.

Durga Khote

First Actress

(1905–1991)

Durga Khote entered films when girls from good families did not work in films. But when Durga Khote, who belonged to a high-class Brahmin family and was educated, entered the film industry, she not only displayed fearlessness and sheer determination, but also opened the doors of Hindi cinema for girls from a good family background.

Before the entry of Durga Khote into films, female characters in films were played by men. When Dadasaheb Phalke made *Raja Harishchandra*, he wanted a lady to portray the role of Harishchandra's wife, Taramati. But as there were no heroines, he had to select a boy for the role. It was then that Durga Khote decided to enter films. In 1932, when V. Shantaram remade *Raja Harishchandra*, he cast Durga Khote as the heroine.

Durga Khote also did character roles. After *Raja Harishchandra*, V. Shantaram produced *Maya Machand* under the banner of Prabhat Studio and cast Durga Khote as a fearless warrior. She wore the clothes of a warrior, complete with a sword in hand and a helmet on the head. In one scene of the film, a character actor was attacked by an eagle. Durga Khote caught the bird and tried to control it till the trainers of the bird arrived. The role of Durga Khote inspired other actresses to take up such daring assignments. In 1936, Shantaram made *Amar Jyoti* in which Durga Khote played the role of a lady who is harassed and finally revolts against her tormentors.

Durga Khote exploded the myth that the film industry was not a place for women.

Satyajit Ray

World-renowned Director-Producer

(1921–1992)

In 1960 when Satyajit Ray returned to Calcutta, he seemed different from the crowd. Calcutta was the centre of Bengali culture and thought. Most people were influenced by Trotsky or Mao. What put Satyajit Ray apart were his thoughts and stature. At 6 feet 4 inches, he definitely stood apart.

Satyajit Ray was born on 2 May 1921 in Calcutta. In the beginning, Ray's interest was towards commercial arts because he was born into a family associated with arts and literature. His grandfather Upendra Kishore Ray was a writer and illustrator and wrote exciting stories for children. He was also the first to start a high-class printing press in Bengal. His father Sukumar Ray was a writer and illustrator of Bengali nonsense verse. So Satyajit Ray had inherited a rich legacy from his family.

However, his father died when he was just two years old. He was looked after by his mother. He studied in a government school where the medium of instruction was Bengali. In 1936, he joined Presidency College where he was taught English. In 1940, when he completed his graduation, he was fluent in both English and Bengali. At the insistence of his mother, he joined Shantiniketan, the university established by Rabindranath Tagore. It was here that he gained an insight into both Indian and Western culture, something which was to be tapped by him in his later life.

In 1943, he returned to Calcutta and joined J. Walter Thompson, a British-owned advertising agency, as an artist. In his 10-year stint at the agency he rose to the post of art director. He also worked for a publishing house as a commercial illustrator and soon became a leading typographer and book-jacket designer. His two typefaces – Ray Roman and Ray Bizarre – are internationally acclaimed. It was when he was illustrating the novel *Pather Panchali* by Bibhuti Bhushan Bandhopadhay that he toyed with the idea of converting the novel into a full-fledged movie. After working for some time in commercial arts, he went to London. There he had the opportunity to watch films made by contemporaries in Europe and America. It was then that he realised his true love was movies. He began to study and understand the nuances of film-making.

He was encouraged in the pursuit of his ambitions by French director Jean Renoir who was in Bengal to shoot for the film *The River*. The success of *The Bicycle Thief* (1948) by Vittorio De Sica with amateur actors, an offbeat story and minimal finances gave him the inspiration that he too could make movies.

As he was short of finances, he mortgaged his wife's jewellery. He continued with his job and in 1952 started shooting on weekends. In 1955 his movie *Pather Panchali* was released. People admired his work and the film. It received rave reviews from the people of Bengal and the West. The film won a major award at the 1956 Cannes International Film Festival. It is still rated one of the finest movies in the world. Then he made *Aparajita* (1956) and *Apur Sansar* (1959). The three films form a trilogy and revolve around a young boy named Apu who is in search of his identity. It symbolises the plight of an average Indian who is torn between tradition and modernity. In 1957, *Aparajita* won the Grand Prix Award at the Venice Film Festival.

Among his appreciated films are – *Jalsaghar* (1958), *Devi* (1960), *Teen Kanya* (1961), *Kanchenjunga* (1962), *Charulata* (1964), *Nayak* (1966), *Aranyer Din Ratri* (1970), *Ashani Sanket* (1973), *Jana Aranya* (1975), *Ganashatru* (1989), *Shakha-Prashakha* (1990) etc. He made a total of around 36 films. He also made two entertaining films for children – *Parash Pather* (1957) and the musical *Gopi Gyne Baga Byne* (1969), which was based on a story by his grandfather.

Besides being a film producer and director, he was also a good writer and editor. He revived the children's magazine *Sandesh*, which was started by his grandfather in 1913, and edited it till his death. His book *Our Films, Their Films* (1976) is a collection of his film-related articles. He has also written science fiction and detective novels. Among his well-known books are *Kale Aura Ajar, Kanchenjunga, Nayak* (dance ballets), and 12 stories.

Oxford University honoured him with a doctorate. He was the second film personality to receive the award after Charlie Chaplin. In 1967, for his contribution to journalism and literature, he was awarded the Magsaysay Award. In the year 1971, he was honoured with the Star of Yugoslavia award. No one in the film industry has scaled the heights that Satyajit Ray did in terms of eminence, popularity and artistic perfection. In 1985, on the occasion of the second centenary celebrations of the French Revolution, the then President of France, Francois Mitterrand went to Calcutta to present him with the Legion d'Honneur, the highest civilian award of France. As a rare gesture by the Academy of Motion Pictures, he was awarded a special Oscar for lifetime achievement. He was also honoured with the Bharat Ratna the same year.

In 1992, he battled for life for three months at a hospital in Calcutta before departing for his heavenly abode on 23 April. On this sad occasion, the then president said, "Just as the Hooghly River merges with the infinite ocean, Satyajit Ray's life has merged with infinite time. His use of the medium of cinema to spread tolerance is incomparable and will continue to remain so for times to come."

He is universally regarded as one of the three greatest film-makers of all time.

Prithviraj Kapoor

Legendary Film and Theatre Actor

(1906–1972)

With films like Sohrab Modi's *Sikandar* (1941), in which he played Alexander the Great and K. Asif's *Mughal-e-Azam* (1960), in which he played Akbar the Great, Prithviraj Kapoor proved that he was an actor par excellence. But very few people know that he was actually a theatre actor and excelled at that too. He began his acting career in theatres at Lyallpur and Peshawar.

He was the first to adopt a professional technique and attitude in Indian theatre. He named his experimental theatre, Prithvi. His fellow theatre actors say that in 16 years, Prithvi Theatre churned out 2,662 shows and he played the lead role in all of them. Even when he was ill, he was particular about doing his work properly. Holding a show regularly for 16 years is no mean achievement.

When Prithvi Theatre suffered from a serious financial crisis, he moved to films. And he soon became a famous actor too.

Prithviraj Kapoor was born at Peshawar, now in Pakistan. In 1927, after completing his studies, he joined Ardhesir Irani's Imperial Film Company as an extra and soon excelled as an actor. He acted in the first Indian talkie, *Alam Ara* (1931). His greatest asset was his powerful, booming voice. In the 1930s, he starred in many Hindi movies produced by New Theatre, a studio based in Calcutta, as the leading actor. Some of his successful films were *Rajrani Meera* (1932) directed by Debaki Bose, *Seeta* (1934) opposite Durga Khote and *Vidyapati* (1937) directed by Debaki Bose. In 1939, he went to Bombay and joined Chandulal Shah's Ranjit Movietone Company.

Despite his commitment to Hindi cinema, he was involved in the construction of Prithvi Theatre with the aim of promoting Hindi stage productions.

He was nominated twice to the Rajya Sabha. In 1969, he was honoured with the Padma Bhushan.

In spite of suffering from cancer, Prithviraj Kapoor continued to work. Among his last movies were *Awara* (1951) and *Kal, Aaj aur Kal* (1972), both directed by his son, Raj Kapoor and *Aasman Mahal*, directed by Khwaja Ahmed Abbas. *Kal, Aaj aur Kal* featured three generations of the Kapoor family.

Raj Kapoor

The Dream Merchant

(1924–1988)

Raj Kapoor believed that both politicians and film producers are performers. Both sell dreams. A politician sells dreams by promising a better tomorrow for the masses and a film producer sells dreams through his films. Raj Kapoor's films are proof that he never compromised on quality and sets for the sake of money. The production costs were heavy because he always wanted his films to fare well at the box office. His films were a reflection on Indian culture and people. The song *Mera Joota Hai Japani* ("My shoes are Japanese") indicates that though he accepted western culture and lifestyle to some extent, he was an Indian to the core – be it *Awara, Shri 420, Phir Subah Hogi,* and *Jis Desh Mein Ganga Behti Hai.* In films like *Sangam, Prem Rog, Satyam Shivam Sundaram* and *Ram Teri Ganga Maili* the chief protagonists were women who were true Indians to the core.

After watching his movies, film producer-director Kedar Sharma remarked that Raj Kapoor's portrayal of love on screen was like the raw passion of cave people. Film producer-director Mahesh Bhatt said that love scenes in Raj Kapoor's films were like the unsophisticated love of a schoolboy. Films like *Sangam* and *Prem Rog* cannot be classified under any genre. All his movies are timeless and evergreen, providing wholesome entertainment as well as a social message. *Aag, Barsaat, Awara, Shri 420* and *Jaagte Raho* are some of his memorable films.

Raj Kapoor started his career in the 1930s as a clapper-boy for Bombay Talkies and as an actor for Prithvi Theatre. Both the companies were owned by his father, Prithviraj Kapoor. He got his first major break as hero in 1948 with the release of *Aag,* which was also directed and produced by him. In 1950, he set up his own film studio – RK Studio. As a writer, producer and director, he made many films under the RK banner. In 1951 came *Awara* with the leading lady of most of his movies – Nargis. The pair became an instant success. His other notable films were *Barsaat* (1949), *Shri 420* (1955), *Jagte Raho* (1956) and *Mera Naam Joker* (1970).

People began to vie for roles under his banner and thought themselves privileged to be a part of RK films. He also made his heroines like Nargis, Vyjayanthimala, Zeenat Aman, Mandakini *et al.* famous.

Raj Kapoor is known as the showman of Indian films. For his contribution to the film industry, he was honoured with the Dadasaheb Phalke Award. However, during the felicitation ceremony on 2 May 1988 he suffered an acute asthmatic attack and collapsed. He died a month later.

Apart from being a great director, he was also a superb actor. People loved him in his portrayal of a naïve country bumpkin a la Charlie Chaplin.

Raj Kapoor was a fun-loving person. His films were full of life, vigour and passion. He wanted to sell dreams through his movies. He wanted people to forget their woes and go into a world of make-believe for a few hours by watching his movies.

Amitabh Bachchan

The One-man Industry

(Born 1942)

Amitabh Bachchan is known in the Indian film industry as the "angry young man". His genre of movies portrayed the hero as a protagonist who opposed those thoughts and beliefs that were harmful for society. His entry into the Hindi film industry gave a new dimension to Indian cinema and he was able to carve a niche for himself in the entertainment world.

When he came over to Bombay from Calcutta to join films, producers rejected him outright for his thin physique, long bamboo-like legs and baritone voice. Dejected, he thought of returning to the company where he was employed earlier.

It was during this period that he met Jaya Bhaduri (whom he later married) and other friends. Slowly, he started getting a few roles. He made his debut in the film *Saat Hindustani* in 1969, directed by Khwaja Ahmed Abbas. People noticed him after the commercial success of *Anand* (1970). It was Prakash Mehra's *Zanjeer*, however, which finally catapulted him to fame. *Zanjeer* was his 14th film and then there was no looking back.

In other films that followed, the genre of the "angry young man" continued. This not only influenced his male contemporaries, but also his female counterparts. It is because of this that in spite of having to compete with brilliant actors like Naseeruddin Shah, Sanjeev Kumar and Dilip Kumar, Amitabh Bachchan was able to rule the hearts and minds of the audience. With the image of the "angry young man", the down-trodden youth identified with him.

After *Zanjeer* came *Amar Akbar Anthony, Deewar, Sholay, Trishul, Muqaddar ka Sikandar, Kala Pathar, Shakti* and others. That he was a versatile actor was proved by the success of his comedy movies like *Chupke Chupke* and *Namak Halal* and the romantic *Kabhi Kabhi*.

During the filming of *Khuda Gawah* in the mountainous terrain of Afghanistan, half of Afghanistan's air force was sent for the security of the film crew. Even the fundamentalist forces of Afghanistan were impressed by his portrayal of an Afghan.

Before entering films, he also did theatre and worked as a radio announcer for some time in All India Radio.

After *Shahenshah* in 1987 the Bachchan magic failed to light up the screen. But he delivered three hits in the 1990s – *Agneepath, Hum and Khuda Gawah*. Then he took a sabbatical from films. In the late 90s, he returned with *Mrityudaata, Lal Badshah, Bade Miyan Chhote Miyan, Major Saab, Kohraam* etc. None of them reproduced the old magic.

Amitabh Bachchan was born on 11 October, 1942 at Allahabad, Uttar Pradesh. His father, poet Harivansh Rai Bachchan and mother, Teji Bachchan were advocates of modern thinking. During Rajiv Gandhi's tenure as prime minister, Amitabh Bachchan was elected to the Lok Sabha from the Allahabad constituency.

In the year 2000, after he hosted the TV programme *Kaun Banega Crorepati*, Star TV catapulted to the No. 1 slot, dethroning Zee TV. His entry into television changed the rules of the game, disproving the critics' contentions. In a poll survey on BBC, Amitabh Bachchan was named the Star of the Millennium beating top Hollywood legends like Charlie Chaplin, Sir Laurence Olivier *et al.*

His son Abhishek Bachchan married the top film star Aishwarya Rai on 20 April 2007. The couple has a daughter.

Currently he is busy hosting a TV show 'Kaun Banega Crorepati V' in 2011 besides acting in Bollywood and Foreign Films including one actor namely De Caprio of 'Titanic' fame.

M.G. Ramachandran

The Filmi Deity

(1917–1987)

Marathur Gopala Ramachandran was born in Kandy, Sri Lanka. Later his family moved to Tamil Nadu where they lived in poverty. At the age of 6, he joined a theatre group – the Madurai Original Boys – where he learnt acting, dancing and swordplay.

MGR made his screen debut in *Sati Leelavathi* (1936) but his first major breakthrough came with *Rajakumari* (1947). MGR's 1950s screen persona in adventure films constructed an image of political as well as physical invincibility. Often the themes of his films were derived from heroic ballads, which are part of the oral tradition of rural Tamil Nadu. For example, *Madurai Veeran* (1956), one of his most popular films, is based on the legend of Madurai Veeran, a popular deity of southern Tamil Nadu.

In the 1960s MGR turned to more 'realistic' fantasies, mostly in a contemporary setting, often playing someone from the oppressed class – a peasant, taxi driver or fisherman. For millions of fans, his image as the knight in shining armour, saving damsels in distress and being totally dutiful towards his mother, was a reality. He based his popularity on love and respect for the mother tongue, motherland and motherhood. He was considered the champion of lower castes/classes who repelled against their exploitation by the upper castes/classes – in reel and real life.

In *Engal Thangam* (1970) for example, playing a truck driver Thangam, MGR fights, sings, cares for the poor and preaches against smoking and drinking.

MGR's stint in politics was equally successful. He had joined the DMK party in 1953 and remained its member till 1972. He fell out with the DMK chief Karunanidhi and used the DMK's propaganda idiom against the DMK itself in *Nam Naadu*. In 1972, he set up the rival Anna-DMK party. In 1977 his party, renamed the AIADMK, won the state elections in alliance with the Congress (I). MGR became the chief minister of Tamil Nadu and was re-elected for three consecutive terms. He introduced several populist schemes like a mid-day meal for school children.

He survived a bullet wound when shot by fellow actor M.R. Radha in 1967. Despite suffering a paralytic stroke in 1984, he survived for three years.

He was awarded the Bharat Ratna in 1988 (posthumously). When he died in 1987, his funeral procession comprised over two million people!

A temple has been built in Madras with MGR as the deity.

Dilip Kumar

The Tragedy King

(Born 1922)

Dilip Kumar was born Yusuf Khan at Peshawar (now in Pakistan) into an orthodox middle-class Muslim family. Later, his family moved to Bombay in search of a livelihood. After the initial struggle, he was introduced into the world of arc lights and grease paint by the prime actress of those times, Devika Rani. Following his debut in *Jwar Bhata* in 1944, he played a variety of characters during a tremendously successful career of over six decades.

Critics hail him as the monarch of tragedy for his popular portrayal of characters subjected to unhappiness, misfortune and loss of loved ones. In *Devdas* he plays the tragic role of a young man madly in love with a woman who is married to another man. He loses his beloved and follows the path of self-destruction. He continues to love and adore her till his very end. With Raj Kapoor and Dev Anand, he formed the famous star trinity of the 1950s backed by the success of films such as *Andaz, Aan, Daag, Madhumati, Ganga Jamuna* and *Ram Aur Shyam*. His performances in the tragical dramas *Deedar* and *Devdas* are often regarded as the epitome of emoting. He was awarded the Filmfare Best Actor Award eight times. He won it for the first time in 1953 for *Daag,* in 1955 for *Azaad,* in 1956 for *Devdas,* in 1957 for *Naya Daur,* in 1960 for *Kohinoor,* in 1964 for *Leader,* in 1967 for *Ram Aur Shyam* and in 1982 for *Shakti.* He produced only one film in which he acted too. This film, *Ganga Jamuna* (1958), became an all-time hit and won many awards. He is the proud recipient of the Dadasaheb Phalke Award.

The doyen of Hindi films, Dilip Kumar is regarded by many as the greatest actor of Indian cinema and as an institution in acting. He has inspired and influenced many actors of his age.

Till today, many actors idolise him and imitate his style of acting and dialogue delivery. But few have been able to create the same magic on the silver screen, as he did. He played memorable character roles in films like *Vidhata, Shakti, Karma* and *Saudagar.*

He created a hit romantic pair with Madhubala – in real and reel life; the crowning glory being *Mughal-e-Azam* in which he played the role of a besotted Salim. This film became a superhit and created many box-office records.

In recognition of his contribution to the field of entertainment, he was nominated a member of the Rajya Sabha by the Government of India. Today, he is leading a happy retired life with his wife Saira Bano – a leading actress of her time.

Meena Kumari

The Tragedy Queen

(1933–1972)

Meena Kumari was born Mahajabeen in 1933 into an orthodox, lower middle-class Muslim family. She was the second of three daughters of Alibux and Prabhawati. In order to support the large family, she had to work as a child-actress. With *Leather Face* (1939), she began her filmi career at the age of six.

In *Baiju Bawra*, she was given her screen name Meena Kumari. Playing Baiju's self-sacrificing sweetheart Gauri, she won accolades for her captivating expressions while singing *Tu Ganga ki mauj main Jamuna ka dhara* with Bharat Bhushan and then as Baiju's lovelorn beloved crooning *Mohe bhool gaye sanwariya*. With the super success of *Baiju Bawra* she climbed to dizzy heights of fame. In Kamal Amrohi's *Daera*, Meena played Sheetal, a 16-year-old girl given in marriage to an old, ailing man often mistaken for her father. The anguish and agony on her face was heart-rending. She was pearless in expressing emotional turmoils and tribulations of the character she played on screen. Some of her films like *Phool aur Patthar* and *Pakeezah* were big budget films that are among the all-time greats.

A role she played to near-perfection was in the Guru Dutt classic *Sahib Bibi aur Ghulam* (1962), as the *chhoti bahu*. In this film, she rebels against the social and religious milieu, resorts to alcohol and dance and desperately tries to seduce her husband, so that he might remain faithful. The scenes and songs of the film like *Na jao saiyan, chhuda ke bahiyan...* shall ever remain etched in the memories of cine lovers.

Earlier in Bimal Roy's *Parineeta* (1953) too, Meena had played a similar role. She was a blend of devotion, pain and purity on the screen. In *Bhabhi ki Chudiyan* she spends her life and even relinquishes it in catering to the emotional and physical demands of her family. This image is repeated in *Dushman* (1971) and Gulzar's *Mere Apne* (1971), although with an emphasis on righteousness. In the latter, the mother-figure weaves her cleansing magic.

However, her crowning glory came with *Pakeezah* (1972), an immortal film about a virginal dancing girl who maintained her intrinsic chastity despite catching the fancy of all the Nawabs and the nouveau riche of the city.

She was known for romantic liaisons with her co-stars. Meena Kumari was the first recipient of the Filmfare Best Actress Award for the film *Baiju Bawra* (1953) and received it four times in all.

Released in February 1972, *Pakeezah* opened to a lukewarm response but after her death on 31 March 1972, the film went on to become a huge success and has since then acquired a legendary status.

Sporting Legends

Dhyan Chand

Outstanding Hockey Player

(1906–1979)

Dhyan Chand wrote in his autobiography, "It's important all of you realise that I am just an ordinary man." This speaks volumes about his greatness, but also depicts his frustration. It is not surprising that these words should come from someone who led the Indian hockey team and won the first Olympic gold medal in 1928 for India. After achieving this honour for India, he advised his son not to take up the sport as it offered nothing in return.

Dhyan Chand joined the Indian Army as an ordinary soldier and in 1926, after a tour of New Zealand, he was promoted to the post of Lance Nayak. After the 1936 Berlin Olympics, he became a world renowned figure, but on the personal front, he gained nothing from all this publicity.

He wrote in his autobiography *Goal*: "After the tour of New Zealand, I became a household name. I thought I was very lucky, but my illusion was brought to a cruel end when I went to the 1936 Berlin Olympics as captain of the Indian hockey team. I saw that if any German soldier performed well, he would be promoted to the post of lieutenant the very next day. Taking that into consideration, I am sure that Hitler would have made me his Field Marshal."

Dhyan Chand represented India in three Olympic Games – 1928 Amsterdam, 1932 Los Angeles and the 1936 Berlin Olympics. Seeing him play and score goals, it seemed that he held a magic wand. In the 37 matches played, India scored 338 goals out of which Dhyan Chand alone scored 133. In his next tour to New Zealand, he scored 201 goals in 43 matches. The 1936 Berlin Olympics was a memorable moment both for India and

Dhyan Chand. India reached the finals after defeating Hungary 4-0, USA 7-0, Japan 9-0, and France 10-0. In the finals, India defeated Germany 8-1.

There were many myths associated with Dhyan Chand and his game. Some believed that his hockey stick had a magnet, which attracted the ball and helped him score goals. Actually, Dhyan Chand had an inborn talent. He could judge and analyse the next move of players of the opposite team just as a skilled chess grandmaster anticipates the moves of his opponents and plays accordingly.

He was conferred the Padma Bhushan in 1956.

Sunil Gavaskar

Outstanding Opening Batsman

(Born 1949)

Sunil Manohar Gavaskar was one of the most outstanding openers in the history of Test cricket. In 1971, he was selected for the West Indies tour. He amassed 774 runs at an average of 154.80 on the tour. India defeated West Indies and later, England. In 1976, India defeated New Zealand and in 1978, Australia, on their home ground. India emerged victorious in all these matches because of the splendid performances by Gavaskar. The 1971 victory was the first away from home after 40 years. In a career spanning 16 years, Sunil Gavaskar captained the Indian team in 46 Test matches.

Sunil Manohar Gavaskar was born on 10 July 1949. He started playing under the guidance of his uncle Madhav Mantri, who was himself a Test-playing cricketer. He was nicknamed "Little Master" for his short stature.

He holds the record for the most centuries – 34, of which 16 were scored against the formidable West Indies. This is an amazing record. He took 100 catches too. He is the only Indian to have scored two centuries in a Test match thrice. He was also the first player to score 10,000 runs in Test cricket.

What is special about Sunil Gavaskar is that he displayed a great deal of strength and stability while playing the game. He also infused his team with confidence.

After his retirement from cricket, he writes columns in newspapers and works as a commentator on TV. After proving himself in the game of cricket, he has now earned fame as a cricket columnist and commentator.

P.T. Usha

Sprint Queen of India

(Born 1964)

Usha's name is a force to reckon with because she practised hurdles by jumping over the walls of her house and broke into the field of athletics, which was then a male bastion. In fact, the credit of inspiring other women to take up sports goes to P.T. Usha. She had her first brush with success and fame at the 1982 Asian Games held in New Delhi, where she won two silver medals.

However, success eluded her at the 1984 Los Angeles Olympics, where she failed to secure the bronze by one-hundredth of a second. She was the first Indian woman to reach the finals of an Olympic event. Although she finished fourth, she set an Asian record of 55.42 seconds for the 400m hurdles. In the Asian Track and Field Championships held at Djakarta, Indonesia in 1985, she won the 100m, 200m, 400m, 400m hurdles and 4 × 400m relay. The record of winning five golds in a single international meet earned her the title of 'India's Golden Girl'.

At the X Asian Games held in Seoul in 1986, she again shot into prominence. She won the 200m in 23.44 secs, 400m in 52.16 secs and 400m hurdles in 56.06 secs. She also earned a name for herself in the 4 × 400m relay race. After the Seoul Asian Games, she returned home with four gold and one silver medals. In the Asian Track and Field Meet held in 1989, she was adjudged the best female athlete.

In spite of putting up a good performance at the Olympics, like Milkha Singh, she was not able to win any medals. But she became a source of inspiration to other women athletes.

Pilavullakandi Thekkeparambil Usha, or simply P.T. Usha, was born at a seaside village called Payolli in Kerala on

27 June 1964. The little girl loved to run on the beach. At the age of 13, Usha joined the government-run sports school at Cannanore. It was here that O.P. Nambiar spotted her potential and took her under his wing.

After marriage in 1991, she discontinued participation in sports for three years. Encouraged by her husband, when she returned to the arena in 1994 to compete as a veteran at the Asian Track and Field Event held in Japan in 1998, she won two bronze medals. She has till now won 102 international medals. At the Asian Games held in Japan, she won two medals. She has thus proved that marriage has not dampened her spirit to succeed in the game.

P.T. Usha was awarded the Padma Shri in 1984 and also received the Arjuna Award in the same year.

Viswanathan Anand

Chess Grandmaster

(Born 1969)

Viswanathan Anand is one player who has strived on his own to put India on the international chess scene. He became a grandmaster at the age of 17. At the age of 27, he became the world's number 2 chess grandmaster.

Anand was introduced to the game at the age of six by his mother. Born on 11 December 1969 in Madras (now Chennai), Anand soon learnt the nuances of the game and was nicknamed "the lightning kid" for his quick moves. At the age of 14, he won the National Sub-Juniors Championship. In 1987, he won the World Junior Championship in Philippines. The following year he was awarded the grandmaster title – the first Indian to achieve this. In 1997 he was awarded the Chess Oscar. In 1999 he was ranked world number two, second only to Garry Kasparov. He was the second non-Russian to come close to winning the title after Bobby Fisher in 1972. He once said, "I play chess to win, but more importantly because I love the game."

In recognition of his outstanding performances, the government conferred the Arjuna Award in 1985, the Padma Shri in 1988, and the Padma Bhushan in 2000. Padma Vibhushan, the second highest civilian award in India was awarded to him in 2007. He wrote a book, *My Best Games of Chess*, a collection of 40 of his best games. It received the 'Book of the Year Award' in 1998 from the British Chess Federation.

Anand won the FIDE world chess championship in 2000 for the first time; and was joint 2nd in 2005. He again won the world chess championship in 2007 (Mexico City, Mexico), in 2008 (in Bonn, Germany), in 2010 (Sofia, Bulgaria) and in 2012 will defend his title in Moscow (Russia) against Boris Gelfand, the winner of candidates matches 2011.

Success and titles have not made him proud or arrogant. He is very polite and humble and personally attends to the e-mails sent by ardent fans.

Sachin Tendulkar

Master Blaster

(Born 1973)

Sachin Tendulkar was just on the threshold of manhood when the world began to compare him with the greatest Australian cricketer Sir Donald Bradman.

Sachin Ramesh Tendulkar was born on 24 April 1973. He learnt the nuances of the game from his coach, Ramakant Achrekar, at a very young age. He made his debut at the age of 16 in Pakistan in 1989 – the youngest player to play Test and one-day cricket. He surpassed many records of batting wizards like Sunil Gavaskar, Vivian Richards, Javed Miandad and others.

Sir Donald Bradman paid the highest tribute to him when he said that among all the players who played international cricket in the past 50 years, it was Sachin Tendulkar who came the closest to his batting style. The records he has established rank him as one of the greatest batsmen of the game. Indeed, *Wisden* (the Bible of cricket) has rated him the second best batsman of all time in Test cricket (after Don Bradman) and one-day cricket. Until now he has scored 51 centuries in Test cricket, beating the record of 34 Test centuries by Sunil Gavaskar, and 48 centuries in one-day international matches. He is the only player to score a double Century in one day internationals.

Apart from being a good batsman, he is also a good bowler and is known to break batting partnerships. The fact is that Tendulkar's game is both impressive and incomparable. When he is on the field, millions of Indians wait with bated breath. He has received countless awards, honours, prize money and cars.

Sachin Tendulkar, to date has amassed more than 15000 runs in Test Cricket and 18000 runs in one-day internationals.

Mihir Sen

Champion Swimmer

(1930–1997)

What Mihir Sen achieved in his time in international swimming is significant, although the records he created have been subsequently bettered. In 1966, he established five important records and became an extraordinary salt-water swimmer. He was the first Asian to have crossed the English Channel. In 1959, he was awarded the Padma Shri and in 1967 the Padma Bhushan.

In 1958, Mihir Sen swam across the English Channel. In 1966, he crossed the Palk Strait, followed by the Strait of Gibraltar, the Bosporus Canal and the Panama Canal. Thus, he established records in long-distance swimming.

Mihir Sen was born on 16 November 1930 in Purulia (West Bengal). He was a lawyer by profession, a barrister of the Calcutta High Court. He was a peerless swimmer, having swum more than 600 kilometres in sea/ocean water. He brought glory to his motherland by creating records and earning a place in *The Guinness Book of World Record*. He died in 1997 after a brief illness.

Kapil Dev

Outstanding All-Rounder

(Born 1959)

Kapil Dev has been India's finest all-rounder in cricket. On January 30 1994, he became the most successful bowler with 431 wickets after the Bangalore Test against Sri Lanka. With this, he equalled the world record of New Zealand's Sir Richard Hadlee who too has 431 wickets to his credit.

When Kapil Dev was just 20, he set a new record of scoring 1,000 runs and taking 100 wickets. He made this record within a period of one year and 109 days only. He started playing first-class cricket in 1975. The opportunity to play in a Test match for the first time came in 1978, during India's tour to Pakistan. The main credit for India's victory at the 1983 World Cup in England goes to Kapil Dev. He was recently honoured with the Wisden Indian Cricketer of the Century Award.

Kapil Dev Nikhanj was born on 6 January 1959 in Haryana. His family dealt in the timber business and later settled in Chandigarh. Kapil Dev did not play cricket until he was 13. He got a break when his name was included in the Sector 16 cricket team as a substitute. Kapil Dev has written his autobiography titled *By God's Decree.*

He has achieved the unique feat of scoring 5,226 runs and taking 434 wickets in 131 Test matches, the first-ever Indian player to do so. He has since retired from professional cricket. Although his name was cited in the match-fixing controversy, he came out unscathed, as the charges could not be substantiated.

Miscellaneous

Jamnalal Bajaj

Freedom Fighter, Social Worker and Industrialist

(1889–1942)

Jamnalal Bajaj was the founding father of the Bajaj Group. The adopted 'fifth' son of Mahatma Gandhi, and the 'merchant prince' who held the wealth he created in trust for the people of his country. Trust – a simple word that contains a whole philosophy handed down by Jamnalal Bajaj to his successors. He valued honesty over profit, actions over words and common good over individual gain.

Jamnalal was born on 4 November 1889, at Kasi-Ka-Bas village in Jaipur State (now the state of Rajasthan). His father Kaniram was a poor man. His mother's name was Brindibai. Jamnalal's father Kaniram had a distant but millionaire relation named Seth Bachhraj of Wardha. He had a widowed daughter-in-law who had no issue. Seth Bachhraj accompanied by his wife Sadibai once visited Kaniram's house, when they were looking for a suitable child for adoption in the family.

Attracted by Jamnalal, Sadibai asked Brindibai to allow her to adopt the child. With utmost reluctance, Jamnalal was allowed to go to Seth Bachhraj as his adopted son, at the age of four. Kaniram stoutly resisted Seth Bachhraj's offer to compensate him for this adoption and asked him to sink a well for the village in lieu of this gesture.

Jamnalal was married at the age of 13 to Jankidevi, daughter of Seth Girdharilal Jijodia of Jaora in Indore State (now the state of Madhya Pradesh). Seth Girdharilal was a wealthy businessman of Jaora. Jankidevi was then only nine years old. The marriage was a typical case of child marriage, so common in those days.

From 1896, when Jamnalal was seven, he was sent to school. He picked up the three Rs and acquired a nodding acquaintance with the English language. His education was through the medium of Marathi, but he achieved workable mastery over Gujarati, Hindi and English as he grew in years.

Jamnalal felt attracted to a number of eminent leaders in public life. He met Pandit Madan Mohan Malaviya. He spent some time with Rabindranath Tagore. He came in contact with Lokmanya Tilak whose journal, *Kesari*, he had been reading since childhood. He appreciated the assertive tone of Tilak's writings. But Jamnalal's spiritual thirst for a guide and guru could only be slaked by Gandhiji.

After the death of Seth Bachhraj, Jamnalal always felt that he had no moral right to enjoy the wealth. He kept his wealth as a 'trust'. In 1908 Jamnalal became an Honorary Magistrate. Ten years later he was given the title of Rai Bahadur. In 1915 he met Gandhiji and felt that he had at last found his spiritual guide. Gandhiji was also attracted to this earnest young man.

In 1920 Jamnalal took a momentous decision which was to change the whole course of his life. He decided to request Gandhiji to treat him as his 'fifth son'. Gandhiji was at first surprised by this strange request, but he gladly agreed to it.

He functioned as the Treasurer of the Indian National Congress practically throughout his life. In 1921 he joined the Non-cooperation Movement and founded the Satyagraha Ashram at Wardha under the guidance of Acharya Vinoba Bhave. In this very year he surrendered the title of Rai Bahadur in pursuance of a resolution passed by the Congress.

In 1923 Jamnalal Bajaj led the National Flag Satyagraha at Nagpur and was sentenced to 18 months' imprisonment. In 1924 he founded the Gandhi Seva Sangh. He also founded the Sasta Sahitya Mandal, which now has its head office in Delhi. It publishes cheap national books in Hindi.

Jamnalal Bajaj also carried on his noble work for the uplift of Harijans. He became the Secretary of the Anti-untouchability Committee of the Indian National Congress and conducted incessant propaganda in favour of the right of Harijans to enter temples. In 1928 he threw open his own Lakshminarayan Temple at Wardha to the Harijans. In 1930 he was elected leader of the Salt Satyagraha Camp at Vile Parle, Bombay.

In 1936 Jamnalal Bajaj gave Segaon village as a gift to Gandhiji who named it 'Sevagram' and founded his ashram there. In 1938 he was elected president of the Jaipur State Praja Mandal. In 1939 he was interned in Jaipur in consequence of the satyagraha campaign in the State for democratic rights. In 1941 he was arrested for anti-war propaganda during the Individual Civil Disobedience Movement. In 1941 he founded the Gouseva Sangha at Wardha for the service of cows.

On 11 February 1942 Jamnalal Bajaj died all of a sudden on account of haemorrhage due to high blood pressure. Mahatma Gandhi in his article in the *Harijan* after the death of Jamnalal Bajaj wrote: "Never was a mortal blessed with a 'son' like him... There is hardly any activity of mine in which I did not receive his full-hearted co-operation and in which it did not prove to be of the greatest value."

Amartya Kumar Sen

Renowned Economist

(Born 1933)

Dr Amartya Kumar Sen, noted economist and philosopher, defied some of the popular 'theories' or 'laws' of economics. And when the Royal Swedish Academy awarded him the Nobel Prize in Economic Sciences for 1998, it recognised his work, especially his studies on famines and his "key contributions to welfare economics". He was the first Asian economist and the sixth Indian to receive the Nobel Prize.

According to well-known British economist Thomas Malthus famine, disease and war were the result of overpopulation. But when Amartya Sen analysed the causes of famine and starvation, he came to the conclusion that shortage of food supply was not just the cause of famine, other factors also contributed to it. Perhaps he was inspired to take up economics because he was himself a witness to the Bengal Famine of 1943. He believed that the famine was the result of man himself rather than natural causes. As a young boy of ten then, he recalled, "The streets were full of emaciated looking faces and people were dying in very large numbers. It made me think about what causes famine. Thirty years later, I was still quite haunted by the memories of that period."

Amartya Kumar Sen was born at Shantiniketan, as his father was working there. In fact he was given the name 'Amartya' or 'the one who deserves immortality' by none other than Rabindranath Tagore himself. Rabindranath Tagore had predicted that the child would go on to earn a lot of fame and recognition for himself and the country.

He studied at Shantiniketan and topped in his intermediate examination. In 1953, he joined Presidency College in Calcutta for his graduation in economics. Then he went to England and joined Cambridge University for his post-graduation and doctorate. When he came back to India, he joined Jadavpur University as professor of economics. He was then just 24.

In 1963 he moved on to Delhi School of Economics (DSE), where he taught for eight years. His fellow professors were V.K.R.V. Rao and K.N. Raj, who were renowned economists. He was associated with DSE till 1971. Then he shifted base to England and joined London School of Economics. He later moved on to Oxford as professor of economics and philosophy. He stayed there for almost a decade before taking over as Master of Trinity College at Cambridge.

Dr Sen has authored about 21 books and over 200 research papers and articles. He has tried to analyse the relation between poverty and famine. Basing his research on the Bengal Famine of 1943, he came to the conclusion that famines are actually man-made catastrophes and not natural disasters. According to him, the famine was the result of the poverty prevalent in the area. The poor did not have the buying capacity. When the prices of food grains soared and the poor did not get a raise in their salaries or supplement their income in some other way, they had to starve. Dr Sen also proved that the main reason behind poverty was illiteracy.

Amartya Sen was married to Navnita Dev in 1960. She is a famous Bengali writer. They were divorced in 1974. They have two children. In 1977, he married a student of DSE named Eva, but she died in 1985. Then he went to England to join London School of Economics. When he joined Trinity College, he met Emma Rothschild who was also teaching there. He later married her.

In recognition of his work, in January 1999, the Indian Government honoured him with India's highest civilian award, the Bharat Ratna.

Tenzing Norgay

Pioneer Conqueror of Everest

(1914–1986)

Standing 8,848m tall, Mt Everest in the Himalayan mountain ranges is the highest mountain peak in the world. On 29 May 1953, Tenzing Norgay, along with New Zealand's Edmund Hillary, became the first to conquer Everest. For more than 50 years, expeditions were being undertaken to conquer the world's highest peak. Many even gave up their lives vying for the honour of being the first to conquer Everest. It remained insurmountable till 1953, when Norgay hoisted the tricolour on the peak.

Tenzing Norgay – originally Namgyal Wangdi, meaning, 'Wealthy, Fortunate Follower of Religion' – was born on 15 May 1914 at Solo Khumbu in Nepal. No one could have guessed that the eleventh child amongst 13 children of an unknown man who lived at Thami village in the district south of Everest could go on to create history. The village was inhabited by *sherpas* (Nepalese people skilled in mountain climbing who primarily work as porters for mountaineers).

As a young boy he ran away from home and settled in Darjeeling, West Bengal. In 1935, he joined Sir Eric Shipton's expedition to Everest as a porter. After the Second World War, he became a *sirdar*, or organiser of porters.

In 1953, he accompanied the British Everest expedition as a *sirdar*. He formed the second summit pair with Edmund Hillary. On 29 May 1953, at 11:30 a.m. they reached the summit. Tenzing Norgay spent 15 minutes on the summit. As a devout Buddhist, he left an offering of food on the summit.

He was considered a hero both in India and Nepal. A controversy brewed about his nationality, but Tenzing silenced it by saying:

"It's true that I was born in Nepal, but was reared and looked after by India."

Pt Nehru congratulated him and helped him set the Mountaineering Training Institute and appointed him the director. He served the Institute till the end. He shared his experiences with aspiring mountaineers at the Institute. When the Institute was inaugurated, Pt Nehru remarked, "This Institute will now produce thousands of Tenzings."

Tenzing believed that for achieving success in any arduous job, one should display immense courage, perseverance, intellect and the potential to face difficult situations. It is because of these inborn qualities in him that Tenzing went on to conquer Everest.

Tenzing was awarded the Padma Bhushan by the President. The Queen of England bestowed on him the George Medal while the Nepal Government conferred on him the title *Nepal Tara* (Star of Nepal).

Tenzing Norgay died on 9 May 1986 in Darjeeling.

Sam Manekshaw

India's First Field Marshal

(1914–2008)

General Manekshaw's name figures prominently in the list of important personalities of the 20th Century. This is because during his tenure in the army, many critical moments came up where the Indian Army had the chance to display their undaunted courage, valour and loyalty. The Indian Army is considered one of the outstanding armies of the world.

Sam Hormuzji Framji Jamshedji Manekshaw, popularly known as Sam Manekshaw, was born in Amritsar on 13 April 1914. Serving in the army had been a passion that he nurtured from childhood. After passing out from Sherwood College, a school in Nainital, he appeared for the army entrance examination. He was one among the 15 candidates finally selected from 12,000 applicants. In 1934, at the age of 20, he passed out from the Indian Military Academy at Dehradun.

On his first assignment, he had to fight the Pathans in the North-West Frontier Province. When the Second World War was at its peak, Sam Manekshaw was sent to Rangoon (now Yangon) to defend Burma (now Myanmar) against the Japanese. The Indian and Japanese army had a confrontation at Sitang Bridge. If the Japanese had been successful in capturing the bridge, it would have become easier to enter India. So Indian forces had to defend it with all their might. Young Manekshaw showed undaunted courage and thwarted the efforts of the Japanese. In the event, the young Captain received six bullets in his stomach. It could have been the end of his dream, but he made an amazing recovery and was awarded the Military Cross for his gallantry.

In 1947, when India was attacked by Pakistani mercenaries, Sam Manekshaw was given the onus of stopping them from advancing on Indian soil. Manekshaw was a good strategist and always drew his plan of action and discussed it with the concerned minister. However, when he discussed the Chinese incursion into India in 1959, his strategy was rejected by the then defence minister V.K. Krishna Menon. But during the Chinese aggression, Sam Manekshaw was asked to thwart it.

Even in the 1971 war with Pakistan, Sam Manekshaw displayed immense valour and led India to a tremendous victory.

For his commendable services to the nation, he was awarded Padma Vibhushan in 1972 and also made the first Indian Field Marshal on 1 January 1973. Throughout his scintillating career that spanned over 40 years, he overawed generals, statesmen, politicians and soldiers alike. The British Commander-in-Chief of the Indian Army during the Second World War, General Sir Roy Butcher, while praising Manekshaw's dedication and valour, said, "The very best staff officer I ever had."

After retirement, Manekshaw had settled down at Coonoor in the Nilgiris. He keeps himself busy by tending cows, bees, poultry and tea plantations. Be it on the battlefront or homefront, for a strict disciplinarian, life knows no difference.

Sam Manekshaw died at the Military Hospital in Wellington (Tamil Nadu) on 27 June 2008 at the age of 94 due to complications arising out of pneumonia. Adjacent to his wife's grave, he was laid to rest in Ootacamund, Tamil Nadu, with full military honours,

Salim Ali

The Birdman of India

(1896–1987)

Dr Salim Ali was one of the world's leading ornithologists. Ali's passion for bird-watching was so strong that he would travel to even the remotest places to pursue his hobby, earning him the title of the Birdman of India.

Dr Salim Ali was born on 12 November 1896 in Bombay. He was initiated into this hobby because of an incident that happened when he was just ten. He shot a sparrow with his air-gun, but the bird seemed unusual. It had a yellow patch on the throat. He wanted to identify it, so he went to the Bombay Natural History Society for this. He was surprised that there were about a dozen species of sparrows and this particular species was one.

Salim Ali wanted to take up ornithology – the study of birds and bird behaviour – so he went to Berlin to study it. Back in India he observed birds in their natural habitat. He made many new and interesting observations about birds. In *The Book of Indian Birds*, he wrote about his observations and gave a boost to bird-watching in India. He co-authored *The Handbook of the Birds of India and Pakistan* with Dr S. Dillon Ripley, which documents observations about more than 2,000 birds in the subcontinent.

In 1976 he was honoured with the Padma Vibhushan. This year, he also won the J. Paul Getty Wildlife Conservation Prize. Dr Salim Ali encouraged bird-watching among the people. He said, "All that you need is an inexpensive pair of binoculars, a notebook, a pencil and an ample stock of patience and dedication." He was an active campaigner for bird conservation in the country.

The renowned ornithologist passed away on 27 July 1987.

Dr Verghese Kurien

Father of the White Revolution

(Born 1921)

Dr Verghese Kurien is the man behind the success of Operation Flood, the movement that helped treble the country's milk production, making it self-sufficient in the production of milk and milk products.

India is a land of villages and a majority of the farmers of these villages keep milch cows and buffaloes. They sell the milk in towns and cities. India leads in the production of milk, but as the villagers were not working in cooperation with each other, they did not benefit from the sale of the milk. This also affected the production of milk. Verghese Kurien formed a co-operative society of such farmers that not only took care of poor, marginal farmers, but also inspired them to expand their business. In this way he laid the foundation of the dairy industry.

Kurien studied engineering at the Michigan University in America. Back in India in 1949, he took up a job at Anand in Gujarat. His dream of improving the farmers' lives was fulfilled by the milk co-operatives. Today, the Anand Co-operative is a well-known industry and the name AMUL is famous the world over.

Very few people know who really was the inspiration behind the co-operative movement. It was Sardar Patel who first worked towards the betterment of the farmers of the area. Later he entrusted the work of improving the living standards of villagers of Kaira and the adjoining areas to Tribhuvandas Patel, who mobilised milk producers into cooperatives.

When Verghese Kurien went to Anand, he changed the concept of dairying. He established a network of veterinary services and cattle-breeding centres. In 1965 he took over as the head of the National Dairy Development Board. He proposed establishing the 'Anand Pattern' all over the country. In 1970 came Operation Flood – a movement that involved 170 million people. It has the credit of being the largest dairy development network in the world. Around six million dairy owners belonging to 75,000 village cooperatives supply milk to 500 towns and cities. Operation Flood has helped stabilise milk prices in the country and ensure the supply of fresh, hygienic milk. India has ceased to depend on milk imports and the co-operative provides a source of regular income to the farmers. Apart from whole and skimmed milk, Anand produces condensed milk, butter, cheese and cheese spreads.

Verghese Kurien has been honoured with several national and international awards. The awards include the Padma Shri, the Padma Bhushan, the Magsaysay Award, the World Food Prize and the Padma Vibhushan. But Verghese Kurien is a modest man. He says that he owes his success to the farmers of Gujarat.

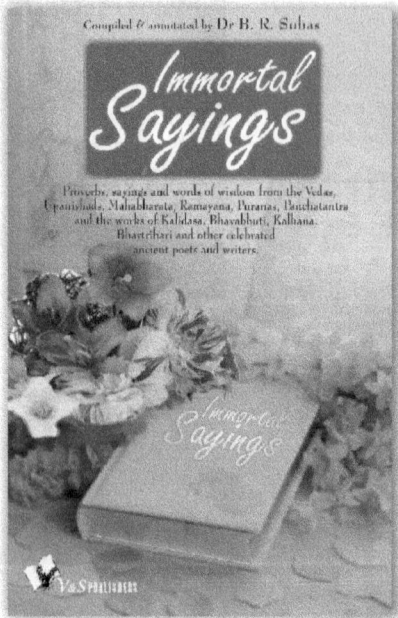

Immortal Sayings

Author: Dr. B. R. Suhas
Format: Paperback
Language: English
Pages: 187
Price: ₹ 125.00

WORLD-FAMOUS SCIENTISTS

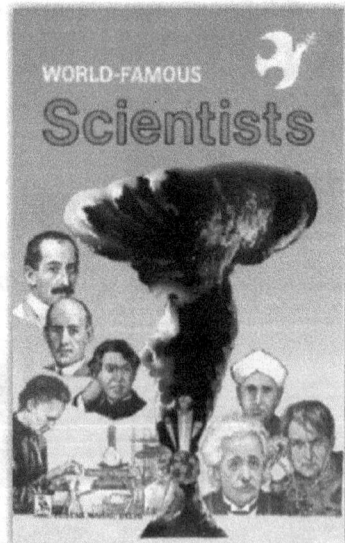

Author: Dr. B. R. Suhas
Format: Paperback
Language: English
Pages: 120
Price: ₹ 80.00

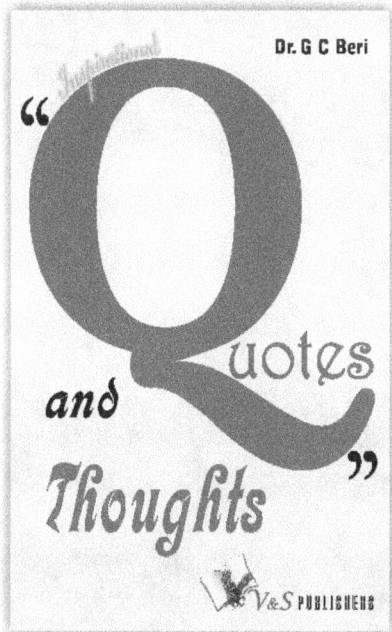

Inspirational Quotes and Thoughts

Author: Dr. G C Beri
Format: Paperback
Language: English
Pages: 104
Price: ₹ 80.00

IMPROVE YOUR WORD POWER

Author: Clifford Sawhney
Format: Paperback
Language: English
Pages: 232
Price: ₹ 88.00

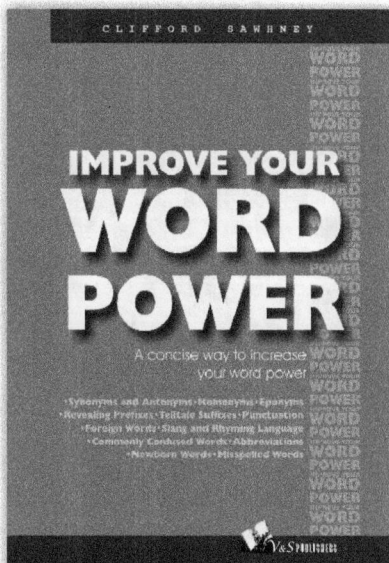

www.ingramcontent.com/pod-product-compliance
Lightning Source LLC
Chambersburg PA
CBHW07041270326
41926CB00014B/2787

* 9 7 8 8 1 9 2 0 7 9 6 8 4 *